Make it Easy
COOKBOOK

Foolproof, Stylish and Delicious Make-Ahead Recipes

Jane Lovett

IMM lifestyle books™

Read. Learn. Do What You Love.

For John, Flora, Freddie and Lucy

acknowledgements

This book has only come to fruition with the help of many people along the way. Heartfelt thanks to you all…

Carola Mangnall, who began the chain which led to its publication by kindly introducing me to my wonderful agent Heather Holden-Brown, and Harriet Benson, for persuading Heather to travel north to witness a demonstration. I am truly indebted to Heather and thank her so very much for her kindness, enthusiasm and encouragement, for holding my hand and making it all such fun.

Clare Sayer, my commissioning editor, for being such a wonderful, sympathetic and relaxed editor and believing in the book in the first place. Tony Briscoe, for taking the beautiful photographs and being so patient, and David Rowley, for his marvellous design. Colleen Dorsey, the amazing editor at Fox Chapel who has overseen this new edition within the tiniest timescale imaginable with great efficiency, patience and good humour, as have all the team at Fox Chapel.

My very dear oldest friend, and assistant extraordinaire, Sally Poltimore, whose contribution to the demonstrations is invaluable and who also makes it all such fun.

My lovely friends and recipe testers Vicky Kirkup and Amanda Finley. Their wise suggestions and observations have greatly improved many of the recipes.

My fantastic back-up team at home whom I couldn't possibly have managed without — Anne Grecian, for patiently and painstakingly checking every recipe with toothcomb accuracy and backing my life up generally. Brenda Izats, for tirelessly, efficiently and good-humouredly assisting me with the endless demonstrations we have done together; and Alison Inness, whose input to and help in the garden I couldn't possibly manage without. I am eternally grateful to you all and also to everyone who has kindly attended demonstrations over the years.

Finally, biggest and best thanks to my chief tasters, John, Flora, Freddie and Lucy, my fantastic family, who are always so encouraging and supportive and whom I love cooking for best of all.

Published 2016—IMM Lifestyle Books
www.IMMLifestyleBooks.com

IMM Lifestyle Books are distributed in the UK by Grantham Book Service.

In North America, IMM Lifestyle Books are distributed by
Fox Chapel Publishing
1970 Broad Street
East Petersburg, PA 17520
www.FoxChapelPublishing.com

ISBN 978 1 5048 0054 9

Printed in China
10 9 8 7 6 5 4 3 2 1

Cover recipe: Oriental Salad, page 135.

contents

introduction

Cooking should be fun...

The question I am asked more than any other when giving cookery demonstrations, is 'when are you going to write a book?', closely followed by 'how far in advance can I prepare this recipe?' and 'how do you sharpen your knives?'.

Well, here is the answer to the first two. A book for the home cook with the emphasis on get-ahead, easy, seasonal recipes with a contemporary twist.

Cooking in general and entertaining in particular is torture for many people. But sharing good food and wine with family or friends should be one of life's great pleasures and should be relaxing, enjoyable and stress-free. Through my recipes I am trying to inspire and instil the confidence to try any recipe without following it slavishly, to adapt it by using alternative ingredients, to add your own stamp – to have a go.

Getting ahead is a good way of spreading both the load and the pressure if time is short. Most recipes can be prepared stage by stage a day or two ahead. It also gives peace of mind. I can cope with most things if I'm organised but I'm totally flustered if not.

I have a passion for food, cooking and all things culinary which I can only think stems from being greedy! For years I have been developing recipes and scribbling ideas on the back of boarding passes and cheque books whilst on my travels. I like to create uncomplicated, simple but stylish food that is quick to prepare using the best seasonal ingredients that taste and look delicious.

The cookery demonstrations that I give are designed to teach people how to cook easily at home. My recipes appeal to novice and experienced cooks

alike and offer suggestions on presenting food with flair for the family, as well as providing that extra wow factor when entertaining. They are all easy to follow, requiring no great skill or cookery know-how and use readily available ingredients. The 'get-ahead' element allows the cook to relax and enjoy the fruits of their labours.

My formal training focused on traditional cooking but latterly my style has become less complicated, quicker, lighter and more relaxed. I very rarely, for example, make a roux-based sauce these days, preferring to improvise with crème fraîche, mustard and Parmesan cheese. During the course of my cooking career, catering and teaching at Leith's Good Food, testing and demonstrating recipes, I have gleaned, through trial, error and experience, a host of tips, techniques and shortcuts that I pass on in the following recipes. Each one is designed to make life in the kitchen a little easier.

Lastly, don't be put off by the length of some of the recipes. Most are short, but I have included as much information as possible, as well as instructions for getting ahead, plus hints and tips. Similarly, despite first impressions of some of the more elaborate recipes, there are no difficult or long drawn-out cooking techniques. A basic knowledge of cooking is all that is required. Happy cooking!

a visit to my garden

When I don't have my cooking hat on, I dive for my gardening one. I love gardening and find it the perfect antidote to a hot kitchen and all that food! Our garden here at Hetton House, in rural North-umberland in Northern England, includes mixed borders and beds, topiary, trees, and a walled vege-table garden which supplies us with herbs and vege-tables all year round. I love all the seasons for what they are and the way they dictate the food we eat. As well as being a joy, picking and cooking fresh fruit and vegetables provides both inspiration and a starting point for many of my recipes, which are incorporated into the cookery demonstrations I run from home and around the UK. I love assembling informal vases of seasonal arrangements year-round, using wild flowers and branches from the woods and flowers and greenery from the garden, and I have a little rule with myself—that I never, ever, buy flowers for the house! Here in the following pages is a brief snapshot of the garden.

One of four beds in the Yew Garden, this is mainly herbacaeous, and is full of clashing colours; it comes into its own in autumn.

Early morning mist rises from the river Till and the valley that skirts the bottom of the garden. Being at the bottom of a wide valley has many pluses, but, combined with the river, it turns the garden into a frost pocket.

Purple lupins and Nectaroscordum in the Long Border. I love this combination in my favourite colours.

The Paved Garden is where we eat outside. Planted with 'pretties and smellies,' it is my view from the kitchen windows!

Swathes of roses festooned from thick nautical ropes suspended from stone pillars act as a backdrop to the Paved Garden on two of its sides.

Box balls in the Yew Garden give structure in winter, but are time-consuming to clip. A real labour of love!

Beautiful 'Coral Reef,' one of my favourite oriental poppies.

Summer pickings can be so colourful: assorted tomatoes, Pink Fir Apple potatoes, various beans, courgettes and sweet peas.

The long herbaceous border in high summer. I love a herbaceous border, even though they are hard work!

It is wonderful having a productive kitchen garden. Despite that, towards late summer and autumn, when the gluts appear, I truly become a slave to it!

A rhubarb forcer in the kitchen garden surrounded by a variety of veggies. In deepest winter we much enjoy our stash of runner (string) beans!

top tips

● Wrap fresh soft herbs in damp paper towel, and store in a plastic bag or clingfilm in the fridge. This prolongs their life considerably.

● Rub garlicky fingers on a stainless steel sink or saucepan to remove the smell.

● Cut tomatoes with a serrated-edged knife using a gentle sawing motion. This prevents crushing the flesh. Acid in tomatoes blunts a straight-bladed knife.

● Salt breaks down egg whites so add a pinch when whisking and making egg glaze but not to poached egg water. 1 egg white is equal to 30 ml (1 fl oz).

● Stack up puff pastry off-cuts before re-rolling to keep the multi-layer structure in place. Scrunching it up results in pastry that won't rise. Only re-roll once.

● Avoid brushing egg glaze onto cut edges of puff pastry as it will set like glue when it goes into the oven and prevent the pastry from rising.

● When cooking steaks or chops, snip the skin and the membrane underneath it in two places to prevent the meat from curling up.

● To diffuse heat on solid electric or range hobs sit the pan on top of three coins. This is a good way to get a consistent gentle simmer or soften onions without browning.

● Always rest meat after cooking. For large joints, leave to stand for 10 minutes out of the oven to stop cooking and then keep somewhere warm for a minimum of 20 minutes. For smaller cuts, remove from the heat for two minutes and then rest somewhere warm for as long as their cooking time. This gives the juices time to re-absorb and allows the meat to relax, producing more succulent and tender meat.

● Seasoning is very important. Salt brings out the flavour of food and is vital to the success of a dish. Taste and season as you go along. Salt added as an afterthought at the end tastes exactly of that.

● The key to a delicious steak is to rub both sides with salt just before cooking. The juices and salt caramelise on contact with the heat producing a delectable exterior.

● Always leave doors ajar when keeping food warm, to allow steam to escape.

● Store empty containers without their lids to allow odours to escape and keep them fresh. This includes thermos flasks and jam jars.

notes on presentation

Food should please all the senses. In the first instance we eat with our eyes, so presentation is important. It doesn't have to be 'cheffy', just imaginatively presented.

By choosing the right cookware and serving dishes food can be transformed. A stew in a 1970s casserole dish is uninviting, whereas slow-braised oxtail or lamb shanks served on a large platter with a gremolata scattered over the top is a feast for the eyes as well as the taste buds. Serve breadsticks, fruit salad or fresh berries in glass vases.

If the main course is 'meat and two veg', try to serve them arranged artistically together on a beautiful big platter. Alternatively, serve all the vegetables together on one large platter and the meat and potatoes on another. This looks festive, bountiful and generous and shows the food off.

Don't be afraid to mix and match china. Vintage china or glass is a lovely way of serving many starters and desserts. Car boot sales and junk shops are a good hunting ground for such finds.

The size of plate that you choose can make all the difference to the look of the food. Plates shouldn't be overcrowded and any spillages around the rim should be wiped off.

Finally, consider the phrase 'less is more' – garnishes should enhance the food rather than become the main attraction.

cooking for friends— a few dos and don'ts

Cooking for friends can be very stressful! Shopping, cooking, table-laying, washing up and being the all-important host. We have less time than ever before, juggling our busy lives, so we need to keep it simple and get ahead as much as possible so that we can join in the fun as well. To paraphrase a military saying: time spent in preparation is seldom wasted.

do

Plan what to cook and shop as far ahead as possible.

Try out a recipe before letting it loose on guests.

Choose one or even two courses that can be prepared a day or two in advance.

Think of textures and colours when planning the menu.

Prepare recipes, or parts of them, whenever you have a window of opportunity. You don't have to do it all in one go.

Serve nibbles instead of a starter – you'll have less to wash up and it's more relaxed. Or offer cheese after the dessert – another easy option. Arrange on a platter or board with membrillo, fresh or dried figs, grapes, celery or walnuts.

Cheat a little if it helps to make life easier. If Marco Pierre-White can use a stock (bouillon) cube, so can we!

Buy smoked salmon, Parma ham or antipasti as a starter if you can't find the time to cook three courses. Arrange artistically, accompany with some good bread and salad leaves and hey presto!

Lay the table the day before if you have time.

Use a timer. I wander around the house with mine.

Prepare dressings and sauces in advance. This usually enhances their flavour and is another job out of the way.

Wash up as you go along.

don't

Be too ambitious. Your guests have come to see you. You are not a chef, nor are you expected to be.

Choose last-minute fiddly or hot starters or any complicated recipes involving lots of ingredients.

Choose anything that requires cooking from scratch at the last minute.

Forget to seal, griddle or fry earlier in the day so that the smoke and smell have time to dissipate.

Panic whilst adding the final flourish to, or carving the main course. Guests won't notice a slight gap after the starter.

Forget to warm the plates and light the candles before your guests sit down.

general notes

All oven temperatures given assume that food is at room temperature before cooking and are for standard ovens. For fan-assisted ovens cook at a lower temperature according to your oven's manual.

Food to be refrigerated should be covered as soon as it's cold and brought back to room temperature before cooking.

Follow either metric or imperial measurements – do not switch between the two.

Pregnant or elderly people should avoid food containing raw eggs or unpasteurized cheese.

Stock (bouillon) cubes are fine to use if fresh stock is not available. I use 1 cube to 300–425 ml (½–¾ pint) of liquid.

soups & starters

Starters set the scene for what is to come. Their role is to get the taste buds going, so they need to be well seasoned and also to look appealing. A bland starter is a very disappointing thing indeed.

yellow (bell) pepper and mascarpone soup

Delicious served hot or cold and the colour is sublime!

Serves 8

2 tbsp olive oil
1 large onion, roughly chopped
5 yellow (bell) peppers
2 cloves of garlic, roughly chopped
1.2 litres (2 pints) chicken or vegetable
  stock

salt and freshly ground black pepper
110 g (4 oz) mascarpone
fresh parsley or coriander and crème
  fraîche or cream, to garnish (optional)

Heat the oil in a saucepan and add the onion. Cook, stirring occasionally, until beginning to soften. Meanwhile, halve, quarter and remove the seeds and white membrane from the peppers. Cut into rough chunks. Add the peppers and garlic to the onions and continue cooking and stirring until the peppers begin to wilt.

Add the stock and bring to the boil. Check the seasoning, stir and leave to simmer until the peppers are very soft – about 30 minutes.

Liquidise the soup in batches, adding a little mascarpone to each batch and pass through a sieve. Check the seasoning. Chill overnight if making in advance or reheat before serving with sprigs of parsley or coriander and a swirl of crème fraîche or cream.

GET AHEAD
Make 2–3 days in advance, cool, cover and refrigerate or freeze. Once thawed the soup will have separated but will come back together again when reheated and stirred.

HINTS AND TIPS
A bowl of small diced croutons would be a good accompaniment, or try a drizzle of parsley or coriander oil made by whizzing together a handful of either herb with a tablespoon or two of olive oil and a pinch of salt.

chilled cucumber, prawn (shrimp) and mint soup

So easy, this can barely be described as a recipe and it looks very pretty to boot!

Serves 4

1 tbsp vegetable oil
1 small onion, finely chopped
1 large cucumber
1 small clove of garlic, roughly chopped
200 ml (7 fl oz) natural Greek yoghurt
50 ml (2 fl oz) double (heavy) cream
4 fresh mint leaves, plus 4 small
  sprigs to garnish

salt and freshly ground black pepper
225 g (8 oz) peeled prawns (shrimp),
plus a few
  extra to decorate
4 rashers (slices) of pancetta or streaky
  bacon, cooked until crispy, cut into
  long strips
snipped fresh chives, shell-on prawns
  (shrimp) and olive oil, to garnish
  (optional)

GET AHEAD
Make the soup (without adding the garnish) up to two days in advance and keep covered in the fridge.

HINTS AND TIPS
Add a few drops of Tabasco sauce when liquidising the soup for a light spicy flavour and a little heat. For a vegetarian soup substitute diced avocado, mixed with a few finely chopped spring onions and mint for the prawns and pancetta.
  Use oil, not butter when making cold soups, as butter solidifies and leaves unappetising particles on the spoon and the lips.

Heat the vegetable oil in a saucepan, add the onion and cook gently until soft and cooked but not brown. Meanwhile cut off a small chunk of cucumber, dice it finely and reserve for garnish. Peel and roughly cut up the rest.

In a liquidiser (blender) blend the cooked onion and garlic with a few chunks of cucumber until it begins to make a purée. Blend in the rest of the cucumber followed by the yoghurt, cream and mint leaves. Season with salt and pepper and then sieve. Thin with a little cold water if necessary. Chill in the fridge; overnight is best.

Stir in the prawns, ladle into bowls and decorate with the extra prawns, reserved chopped cucumber, pancetta or bacon strips and mint sprigs or chives. The odd drop of olive oil looks very good too.

Cucumbers in the greenhouse

jellied borscht

This is elegant, unusual, inexpensive and healthy and never fails to impress. Piroshkis, little mushroom pastries (see page 16) are the traditional accompaniment to borscht and will add a really special touch to your dinner party. To make things go with a swing, serve your guests with a glass or two of Iced Lemon Vodka (see page 173)!

Serves 8

4 medium raw beetroot (beets), cut into chunks
1 carrot, cut into chunks
1 onion, cut into chunks
1 stick of celery, cut into chunks
8 black peppercorns
3 x 400 g (14 oz) tins of beef consommé

4 leaves of gelatine (for powdered gelatine, see Hints and Tips)
2 tbsp crème fraîche
½ tbsp horseradish sauce
snipped fresh chives or 2 chopped spring onions
50 g (2 oz) jar Avruga or Onuga 'caviar' (optional)

Put the beetroot, carrot, onion, celery and peppercorns into a saucepan. Add the consommé, bring to the boil and simmer for 30–40 minutes until the vegetables are tender. Strain into a bowl.

Soak the gelatine leaves in a bowl of cold water for 3–5 minutes until softened. Squeeze out the excess water with your hands and add to the hot but NOT boiling soup. Stir well, cool, cover and refrigerate until required. Overnight if possible. Mix the crème fraîche and horseradish together in a bowl, cover and set aside.

Using a metal spoon, stir the Borscht round and round in the bowl, until it has all broken up into a softish mass which looks a bit like crushed ice.

Divide the soup between eight soup plates, bowls or cups and top each one with a dollop of the crème fraîche mixture and some chives or chopped spring onions. Finish with the 'caviar', if using.

GET AHEAD
Make to the end of the second paragraph up to 3 days in advance. Borscht freezes beautifully. However, once thawed it needs heating in a saucepan only just until it becomes a smooth liquid again. Do not boil as the gelatine will lose its setting properties. Pour into a bowl, cool, cover and put in the fridge until set. Continue with the breaking up stage.

HINTS AND TIPS
Chill the soup plates, bowls or cups in advance if you have space in the fridge.

To use powdered gelatine instead of leaf gelatine, sprinkle 3 level tsp gelatine over 4 tbsp water in a small saucepan. Leave for a few minutes to sponge/bloom. The mixture will become solid and look like a sponge. Slowly dissolve the gelatine over a very gentle heat. Do not boil. Whisk the gelatine into the soup mixture and continue as directed. If you can, do use leaf gelatine. It is foolproof and much easier than powdered!

piroshkis

These little crescent-shaped pastry savouries are traditionally served with Borscht (see page 14) but also make fabulous canapés.

Makes about 22

30 g (1 oz) butter
1 small onion, finely chopped
2 sticks of celery, finely chopped
110 g (4 oz) flat mushrooms, finely chopped

salt and freshly ground black pepper
ground nutmeg
250 g (9 oz) puff pastry
1 egg, beaten with a little salt

GET AHEAD
Make these a day ahead; simply cover the uncooked piroshkis and keep in the fridge or make further in advance and freeze.

HINTS AND TIPS
Piroshkis make very tasty hot canapés. Some soured cream or crème fraîche mixed with finely chopped spring onions or snipped chives would be good to dip them into.

Preheat the oven to 220°C (425°F) gas 7.

Melt the butter and cook the onion and celery until soft but not coloured – about 5 minutes. Add the mushrooms and cook for another 10 minutes or until the mixture is cooked and all the liquid has evaporated. Season well with salt, pepper and nutmeg and leave to cool.

Roll the pastry out thinly and cut into 7 cm (2¾ in) circles with a plain pastry cutter. Brush each circle with the beaten egg and put a little of the mushroom mixture in the middle of each one – roughly ½ teaspoonful.

Fold the pastry over forming a half-moon shape, seal the edges by crimping with a fork and place on a baking sheet lined with silicone paper. Brush the tops with beaten egg and bake for 5–10 minutes or until golden brown and puffed up.

spinach soup with poached eggs and goats' cheese croûtes

This lovely green soup is very nutritious and a meal in itself when topped with a poached egg and served with goats' cheese croûtes. Adding the spinach to the soup just a few minutes before liquidising means it retains its vibrant colour.

Serves 8

2 tbsp olive oil plus extra for brushing
1 large onion, chopped
1 medium potato, roughly chopped
2 cloves of garlic, roughly chopped
1 tsp finely chopped ginger
1.2 litres (2 pints) chicken or vegetable stock
a grating or pinch of nutmeg
salt and freshly ground black pepper
450 g (1 lb) spinach, washed

cream or crème fraîche (optional)
a splash of white wine vinegar
8 very fresh eggs
8 diagonally cut slices of baguette or ciabatta
8 slices of goats' cheese
fresh thyme sprigs

Heat the oil in a large saucepan, add the onion, potato and garlic and cook until beginning to soften but not colour.

Add the ginger, stock and nutmeg and bring up to the boil. Check the seasoning and simmer for 20 minutes until the potato is cooked.

Add the spinach, stir until wilted and cook for 2 minutes. Purée the soup using a liquidiser (blender) or hand blender, adding some cream or crème fraîche to taste, if using. You might like to save some cream to 'swirl' in just before serving. Pass through a sieve.

Preheat the grill to high. Bring a saucepan of water to the boil. Add the vinegar, swirl the water around with a spoon and drop in the eggs one or two at a time, having first cracked them into a ramekin or cup. Poach for 3 minutes before removing with a slotted spoon and draining on paper towel. Keep warm.

Brush the sliced bread with a little olive oil and salt, grill both sides lightly, top each one with a slice of goats' cheese and a sprig of thyme and grill until golden brown and bubbling.

Ladle the soup into eight bowls and top each one with a poached egg. Serve the croûtes alongside.

GET AHEAD
Make the soup up to 2 days in advance; after sieving, cool, cover and chill. Reheat gently, just before required, remove from the heat when just under boiling point and serve straight away. If left too long in the pan the colour will deteriorate.

Poach the eggs up to a day in advance. When cooked slip them from the slotted spoon straight into a bowl of cold water, cover and chill. To reheat, drain, cover with boiling water and leave for 2–3 minutes to reheat before draining well on paper towel and serving on top of the soup.

HINTS AND TIPS
You may need to thin the soup with a little stock or water.

tom ka gai

I love broth soups. Most are put together from good stock and store cupboard ingredients and the variations are as endless as the imagination. This well-known Thai soup is fresh, zingy, aromatic and warming.

Serves 8–10 as a starter or 4–6 as a main course

2 tbsp vegetable oil
110 g (4 oz) shiitake, chestnut or button
  mushrooms, sliced
1.4 litres (2½ pints) chicken stock
400 ml tin (can) coconut milk
4 spring onions, white part only,
  trimmed and sliced on the diagonal
4 Kaffir lime leaves
2 tbsp fish sauce (nam pla)
2.5 cm (1 in) piece of fresh ginger,
  peeled and sliced into thin batons

1 small red chilli (chili pepper), halved,
  seeded and finely sliced
2 stalks of lemon grass, bruised
1 tbsp palm or brown sugar
juice of 1 lime
1 chicken breast, cut into thin slices
200 g (7 oz) cooked rice noodles
  (optional)
bunch of fresh coriander, leaves and thin
  stems roughly chopped

GET AHEAD
Make in advance to the end of paragraph 2. Reheat then continue with the rest of the method just before serving.

HINTS AND TIPS
Up the quantity of noodles for a more substantial lunch and substitute raw prawns (shrimp) for the chicken if you like. Pak choi or spinach could also be added just before serving.

Heat the oil in a largish saucepan or wok and fry the mushrooms until all the liquid has evaporated. Don't let them brown.

Add the chicken stock, coconut milk, spring onions, lime leaves, fish sauce, ginger, chilli, lemon grass, sugar and lime juice. Stir together, gently bring up to the boil and simmer for a few minutes.

Add the sliced chicken to the broth and simmer for a few more minutes until it has changed colour and cooked through.

If using noodles divide between the individual serving bowls. Ladle the soup into the bowls and scatter with roughly chopped coriander just before serving.

beetroot (beet), hazelnut, goats' cheese and watercress salad

Fresh, earthy and colourful. Try to use fresh raw beetroot (beet) and avoid ready-cooked if you can, and in particular the ones doused in vinegar, as they are generally overcooked and soggy with little flavour.

Serves 4

*340 g (12 oz) small raw beetroot (beet)
  or 225 g (8 oz) ready-cooked
olive oil
salt and freshly ground black pepper
1 large or two small Jerusalem
  artichokes (optional)
a handful of whole blanched hazelnuts*

*4 handfuls of watercress or mixed green
  salad leaves
110 g (4 oz) goats' cheese
hazelnut, cobnut or walnut oil
Balsamic Syrup (see page 178)*

GET AHEAD
Prepare to the end of paragraph 4 up to a day in advance and assemble when required. It can be served with the beetroot and artichokes warm, as well as cold. Just reheat for a few minutes before assembly.

HINTS AND TIPS
Substitute feta cheese for the goats' cheese if you prefer.

Foraged hazelnuts

Preheat the oven to 190°C (375°F) gas 5.

If using raw beetroot, wash and cut off all but 5 cm (2 in) of the stems. This is important; otherwise the beetroot will 'bleed' during cooking. Place in the middle of a large square of foil, scatter over a good glug of olive oil, season and wrap up loosely, forming a large tent. Put onto a baking sheet and cook for 1 hour or until tender. When cool enough to handle slide off the skins, wearing gloves to prevent stained hands. Cut the cooked beetroot in half and then into 6 or 8 wedges depending on their size.

If using, scrub the artichokes, bring up to the boil in cold salted water and simmer for 5–10 minutes, depending on their size, until just tender. Drain, peel and cut into discs. Or slice them, skins on, fry in a little olive oil and drain on paper towel.

Roast the hazelnuts in a dry frying pan until they release their aroma and begin to brown. Set aside.

To assemble, place a handful of watercress or mixed green leaves on each plate and stack the beetroot in the middle, points uppermost. Scatter over the artichoke discs if using, followed by some crumbled goats' cheese and then the hazelnuts. Season with a little sea salt and a swirl of nut oil and some balsamic syrup.

twice-baked roquefort soufflés

A very impressive prepare-ahead starter. For lunch add a chicory (Belgian endive) and walnut salad and some crusty bread. Perfect!

Serves 8

50 g (2 oz) butter, plus extra for greasing
grated Parmesan (optional)
50 g (2 oz) plain (all-purpose) flour
a pinch of mustard powder or a little
  made-up English mustard
salt and freshly ground black pepper
290 ml (½ pint) milk

170 g (6 oz) Roquefort cheese,
  crumbled
4 eggs plus 1 extra egg white
8 tsp double (heavy) cream
a few walnut pieces
snipped fresh chives, optional
Roasted Red (Bell) Pepper Sauce
  (see page 179)

(see page 179)

GET AHEAD
Make soufflés up to three days in advance. After the first baking, turn them out as described, cover and keep in the fridge. Alternatively, wrap individually in clingfilm and freeze. They take no time at all to thaw. Proceed with the recipe after thawing, bringing back to room temperature for at least an hour before cooking.

HINTS AND TIPS
For the best flavour the soufflés need to be well seasoned. You could use ramekins instead of cups.

Preheat the oven to 180°C (350°F) gas 4. Butter 8 round-bottomed teacups or mini pudding basins. Dust with grated Parmesan, if using, tipping out the excess by gently knocking the containers. This adds a nice tasty coating to the soufflés.

Melt the butter in a saucepan, add the flour, mustard, salt and pepper and cook for 30 seconds. Take off the heat, add the milk and incorporate using a small whisk. Return to the heat and whisk until the sauce thickens. It will be very thick. Stir for a further 30 seconds. Remove from the heat and stir in two-thirds of the cheese.

Separate the eggs and stir the yolks into the cheese sauce. Check the seasoning and tip the sauce into a large bowl. Boil a kettle of water.

Whisk the egg whites with a pinch of salt until they are just stiff but not dry. Stir a spoonful of the whites into the cheese sauce to loosen the mixture. Then, using a large metal spoon, very gently fold in the rest of the whites, ensuring that all the mixture is incorporated from the bottom of the bowl.

Spoon the mixture into the prepared cups. Insert a teaspoon or knife into the mixture and draw a circle around the cup to form a 'hat' when the soufflé cooks. Stand in a roasting tin, put into the oven and carefully pour in enough boiling water to come half-way up the sides of the cups.

Cook for 20 minutes or until brown, well-risen and just set in the middle. Remove the cups from the water. Whilst still warm, loosen the soufflés with a round-bladed or palette knife and turn them out onto your hand. Put them into a buttered ovenproof gratin dish or individual ovenproof serving dishes.

Preheat the oven to 220°C (425°F) gas 7. Spoon 1 tsp cream over each soufflé, scatter with the remaining cheese and cook for 10 minutes or until golden and well risen. Serve with scattered walnut pieces and chives and roasted red pepper sauce.

red (bell) pepper terrine

This is a lightly set, airy mousse. It is very colourful, incredibly tasty and is made mainly from storecupboard ingredients. It's especially delicious served with Tapenade Croûtes and Tomato Vinaigrette.

Serves 12

1 onion, roughly chopped
2 tbsp olive oil
2 x 400-g (14-oz) tins (cans) red (bell) peppers or 3 x 290-g (10-oz) jars of roasted red peppers in oil or brine (you need approximately 600 g / 1 lb 5 oz drained weight in all)
2 cloves of garlic, crushed
400 g tin (can) of chopped tomatoes
2 tsp sun-dried tomato purée

1 heaped tsp sugar
3 tbsp red or white wine vinegar
1 tsp salt
freshly ground black pepper
9 leaves of gelatine (for powdered gelatine, see Hints and Tips)
290 ml (½ pint) double (heavy) cream
6 pitted black olives, finely chopped
chopped fresh parsley (optional)
Tomato Vinaigrette (page 179) and Tapenade Croûtes (page 179), to serve

Wet a 1.2 litres (2 pint) terrine or loaf tin and line it with a large piece of clingfilm.

Cook the onion gently in the olive oil until softened but not brown. Meanwhile, drain the peppers. Reserve a quarter of a pepper for decoration and roughly chop the rest. Add to the onion with the garlic, tinned tomatoes (I rinse the tin out with a splash of water and add that too), sun-dried tomato purée, sugar, wine vinegar, salt and pepper. Bring up to the boil, stir well and cook slowly for 20 minutes or until the mixture is soft and pulpy, stirring occasionally. Remove from the heat.

Soak the leaves of gelatine in a bowl of cold water for 5 minutes until softened. Squeeze out the excess water with your hands and then stir into the peppers.

Liquidise the mixture and pass through a sieve. Check the seasoning – it needs to be well seasoned at this point to compensate for the unseasoned cream.

Lightly whip the double cream to the same consistency as the pepper mixture and fold it into the purée. A quick whisk will dispose of any stubborn lumps. Pour into the terrine or loaf tin and when cool, cover and leave to set in the fridge overnight.

Dice the reserved pepper and mix with the olives. You might like to add a little chopped parsley as well which looks very pretty. Turn out the terrine, slice (straight from the fridge) and arrange on individual plates. Spoon a little of the olive mixture on top of each slice, a little puddle of tomato vinaigrette over one corner, decorate with parsley or chives and serve with tapenade croûtes.

GET AHEAD
The terrine can be made 2–3 days in advance and will keep happily covered in the fridge. The olive topping can be made at the same time as the terrine but don't add the chopped parsley until just before serving.

HINTS AND TIPS
The easiest way to line a container with clingfilm is to rinse the inside under the tap first which helps the film stick to the sides. Make sure your hands are dry else it will stick to them instead!

If the jars of peppers have vinegar in the preserving liquid, omit the vinegar from the recipe.

Make in individual moulds and turn out, or individual dishes and don't turn out.

Gelatine loses its setting qualities if boiled so always add it off the heat and when the mixture has had time to cool a little. For vegetarians use agar-agar, the alternative to gelatine.

To use powdered gelatine instead of leaf gelatine, sprinkle 7 level tsp gelatine over 5 tbsp water in a small saucepan. Leave for a few minutes to sponge/bloom. The mixture will become solid and look like a sponge. Slowly dissolve the gelatine over a very gentle heat. Do not boil. Stir into the peppers and continue as directed. If you can, do use leaf gelatine. It is foolproof and much easier than powdered!

oriental beef

One of my most popular recipes, this has to be one of the easiest and most delicious get-ahead starters. Up the quantities and it becomes an elegant lunch, or, swap the beef for salmon, especially if the main course is meaty. Serve with Griddled Bread (see page 176).

Serves 8

2 x 225 g (8oz) fillet (tenderloin) steaks
  or 450 g (1lb) fillet tails
vegetable oil
4 spring onions
2 red chillies (chili peppers)
mixed coloured baby salad leaves
sesame seeds, toasted
sprigs of fresh coriander (optional)

For the dressing
1 tsp finely chopped ginger
1 clove of garlic, finely chopped
1 small shallot, finely chopped
4 tbsp sesame oil
6 tbsp vegetable oil
1 tbsp soy sauce
2 tbsp lemon juice

Trim the beef of any membrane, rub with oil and seal quickly on all sides in a very hot frying pan. Set aside and allow to cool. In a small bowl whisk together all the dressing ingredients. Set aside.

Trim the spring onions and slice very finely into ribbons lengthways. Halve, seed and remove the membrane from the chillies and slice them very thinly lengthways.

Slice the beef very thinly across the grain and arrange in a circle in the middle of 8 plates leaving a space in the very middle.

Just before serving arrange a small handful of salad leaves in the middle of each plate, whisk the dressing and spoon about 2 tablespoons over the beef and salad. Mix the spring onions and chilli together and scatter over the top of the leaves followed by a dusting of toasted sesame seeds and a sprig of coriander, if using.

GET AHEAD
Slice and arrange the beef on plates any time on the day and cover. Stack up in the fridge if more than three hours in advance.

HINTS AND TIPS
Fillet tails are cheaper than steaks, so ask the butcher.
  If you put the sliced spring onions and chilli into a bowl of water in the fridge they will curl up into interesting and attractive shapes! Drain and dry on paper towel before using.
  If substituting salmon use 700 g (1 lb 9 oz) very fresh salmon fillet sliced into 3–5 mm (⅛–¼ in) thick slices, up to a day in advance. Top with a criss cross of fresh chives plus a few extra snipped ones or some fresh coriander leaves followed by the toasted sesame seeds. Don't be put off by the salmon being raw as it 'cooks' in the dressing.

parma ham, mozzarella and rocket (arugula) roulades with basil vinaigrette

The Mediterranean on a plate – simple, fresh and tasty.
I sometimes make these in miniature to serve as canapés,
which is very handy as they can be made the day before.

Serves 8

1 large buffalo mozzarella cheese
16 slices of Parma ham
32 small sun-blush or 16 sun-dried
   tomatoes, halved
2 good handfuls of rocket (arugula)
few capers

For the basil vinaigrette

1 tbsp white wine vinegar
6 tbsp olive oil
salt and freshly ground black pepper
about 20 fresh basil leaves
1 small clove of garlic, roughly chopped
1 small shallot, finely chopped

GET AHEAD
Make the roulades several hours ahead (in the morning for the evening), cover and chill. The basil vinaigrette can be made up to 6 hours ahead.

HINTS AND TIPS
You can use pesto sauce instead of basil vinaigrette. Loosen it with a little olive oil if necessary.
   Parma ham is easier to handle straight from the fridge.

Cut the mozzarella into slices and then into 32 batons. Lay the slices of Parma ham out individually on the worktop.

   Put two batons of mozzarella at one end of each piece of Parma ham, followed by two tomatoes, a few capers and a small bunch of rocket leaves. Roll the roulades up quite tightly, allowing some of the rocket to stick out of the ends.

   Whizz all the vinaigrette ingredients together using a small food processor, an electric hand blender or a pestle and mortar.

   To serve the roulades, place two per person on individual plates, either side by side or one propped up against the other and spoon over a little of the basil vinaigrette. Scatter a few extra drained capers around the plate.

mushroom, thyme and taleggio galettes

Crispy puff pastry bases with a delicious medley of creamy mixed mushrooms on top. If you are lucky enough to have a reliable source of wild mushrooms, all the better!

Serves 6 as a starter or 4 for lunch

30 g (1 oz) butter
1 shallot, finely chopped
225 g (8 oz) mixed mushrooms, sliced
1 clove of garlic, crushed
4 sprigs of fresh thyme
salt and freshly ground black pepper
4 tsp crème fraîche

1 egg yolk
1 tbsp chopped fresh parsley
375 g packet ready-rolled all butter
*   puff pastry*
85 g (3 oz) Taleggio cheese
mustard cress, to garnish

Preheat the oven to 220°C (425°F) gas 7.

Heat the butter in a frying pan, add the shallot and cook until soft but not brown. Add the mushrooms, garlic, the leaves from one sprig of thyme and some seasoning and cook over a high heat until all the liquid has evaporated and the mixture is sizzling again and very dry. Check the seasoning, tip into a bowl and leave to cool. Stir in the crème fraîche, egg yolk and chopped parsley.

Roll the pastry out a bit thinner – about the thickness of a pancake. Cut six 12 cm (4½ in) circles using a pastry cutter or a small saucer as a template. Put onto a baking sheet lined with silicone paper and lightly score a rim 1 cm (½ in) in from the edge. Chill for 30 minutes.

Divide the mushrooms between the pastry discs, spread out leaving the rims clear and top with a thin slice of Taleggio and a small sprig of thyme. Cook for 5–10 minutes or until golden brown and bubbling.

GET AHEAD
Prepare to the end of paragraph 3 up to 2 days in advance, cover individually and keep in the fridge. Both components can be frozen at this point either individually or as fully made-up galettes. Thaw for two hours before cooking.

Assemble the galettes several hours before you want cook them and cover.

HINTS AND TIPS
For lunch make the pastry bases larger – about 13 cm (5 in) and cut out 4 circles.

prawn (shrimp) and smoked salmon terrine

I wanted to make a terrine that wasn't all mayonnaise and gelatine and here it is – stuffed full of prawns (shrimp) which are simply bound together with mascarpone. The 'caviar' is optional, however, do not use Danish lumpfish roe as the dye will run into the terrine turning it black.

Serves 12–16

knob of butter
2 bunches of spring onions, finely chopped
340 g (12 oz) thinly sliced smoked salmon
250 g (9 oz) mascarpone
juice of 1 lemon
4 tbsp snipped fresh chives
12 drops of Tabasco sauce
1 tsp salt

freshly ground black pepper
550 g (1¼ lb) cooked, peeled prawns (shrimp) (800 g / 1 lb 12 oz frozen weight)
1 x 50-g (2-oz) jar of Onuga or Avruga 'caviar', optional

To serve
Pickled Cucumber (page 177), Tomato Vinaigrette (page 179), watercress or some extra chives

GET AHEAD
Make the terrine up to 2 days ahead and refrigerate.

HINTS AND TIPS
Avruga or Onuga Caviar is in fact herring roe and quite delicious. Stored in the fridge, it has a long shelf life so it is very useful to have a jar 'in stock' for decorating canapés or starters.

It is impossible to buy fresh, cooked, peeled prawns. The ones you see in the shops have been frozen and thawed out, for which the shops charge a lot extra, so it is cheaper to buy them frozen and thaw at home.

Cook the onions in the butter gently until soft but not coloured. Allow to cool.

Wet the inside of a 1.2 litre (2 pint) terrine or loaf tin and line with clingfilm, then slightly overlapping slices of smoked salmon, leaving a little hanging over the sides to fold back over the top when filled. Finely chop the rest of the smoked salmon.

In a large bowl beat together the mascarpone and onions. Stir in the lemon juice, chives, chopped smoked salmon, Tabasco, salt and pepper.

Drain the prawns on paper towel and then squeeze gently in your hands to extract the excess moisture but not to dry them out completely. Chop briefly in a food processor or by hand. Don't over-do it, they should still be chunky and have some texture. Mix into the rest of the ingredients. Check the seasoning. You may like to add some more Tabasco.

Finally, stir in the 'caviar', if using, and spoon into the prepared terrine, pressing down as you go. Fold the overlapping smoked salmon over the top, cover and chill overnight. To serve, turn out, remove the clingfilm and slice straight from the fridge. Decorate with chopped chives or watercress and serve with pickled cucumber.

carpaccio of salmon with pink peppercorns

Pretty, elegant, fresh and healthy, this lovely starter is delicious accompanied with toasted sourdough or Griddled Bread (see page 176).

Serves 4

450 g (1 lb) very fresh salmon fillet
½–1 tbsp pink peppercorns
⅛ red onion, very finely sliced or
  chopped (optional)

fresh dill, coriander, chervil or parsley
juice of 1 lime or lemon
salt and freshly ground black pepper
good olive oil

GET AHEAD
You can slice and arrange the salmon on plates up to a day in advance, Just cover with clingfilm and stack up in the fridge.

Slice the salmon very thinly, as though slicing smoked salmon. Discard the dark, fatty tissue that runs close to the skin. Arrange on four dinner plates making sure that the base of each plate is completely covered with salmon.

Scatter over a few pink peppercorns (you might not need them all), a little onion, if using, and tiny sprigs of whichever fresh herb you have chosen.

Just before serving, sprinkle a little lime or lemon juice over the salmon followed by some sea salt and freshly ground black pepper. Finally, with your thumb over the top of the bottle, swirl around a circle or two of good extra-virgin olive oil.

buffalo mozzarella with roast cherry tomatoes and tapenade dressing

An easy, colourful starter or lunch that takes only minutes to prepare. Griddled Bread (see page 176) mops up the tasty juices perfectly.

Serves 4 as a starter or 2 for lunch

16–20 small cherry tomatoes on the vine
2 buffalo mozzarella
salt and freshly ground black pepper
a little olive oil

100 g (4 oz) jar of tapenade
few fresh basil leaves
handful of rocket (arugula) leaves
avocado oil, for drizzling

GET AHEAD
The tomatoes can be cooked up to two days ahead, but warm them through again to freshen them up before using. Serve warm or at room temperature.

HINTS AND TIPS
If serving the tomatoes warm, leave on the baking sheet ready for reheating. Assemble just before serving

Preheat the oven to 220°C (425°F) gas 7.

Snip the tomato vines into four sections (each one should have 4 or 5 tomatoes attached), spread out on a baking sheet lined with silicone paper or foil, scatter with a little salt, black pepper and olive oil and cook for 10–12 minutes or until the skins have burst and the tomatoes are a little charred but still holding together.

Break the cheeses in half and sit them, torn sides down, on paper towel to drain for a few minutes. Tear into chunky pieces and divide between four, stacking them up in the middle.

Arrange a sprig of tomatoes on top (don't worry if the odd one falls off the vine) and dot over a few blobs of tapenade. If you would prefer the dressing to be slightly runnier, thin with a little olive oil. Scatter with one or two torn basil leaves and some rocket leaves over the top – not too many. Finish with a generous swirl of avocado oil and a teaspoon of the tomato cooking juices.

fish & shellfish

I think the less that is 'done' to fish the better – just a few ingredients that complement or perhaps enhance the delicate taste. However, some fish has a more robust taste and texture than others and so can take stronger accompanying flavours.

Always choose the freshest fish possible. Whole fish should be slippery, firm fleshed, the eyes bright and not sunken and the gills bright pink and not brown. Fillets should be firm and translucent with no spots of brown discolouration. Above all, it shouldn't smell at all fishy – just pleasingly of the sea.

swedish salmon

Cooking doesn't get much easier than this. Omit the smoked salmon if you like – it will still be delicious.

GET AHEAD
Make the sauce up to a day in advance, cover and refrigerate.

Serves 4

4 x 140–170 g (5–6 oz) salmon fillets,
  skin on or off
110 g (4 oz) smoked salmon
200 ml (7 fl oz) crème fraîche

3 level tsp Dijon mustard
2–3 tbsp white wine
salt and freshly ground black pepper
2 tbsp fresh chives or dill

HINTS AND TIPS
Add the herbs at the very last minute as otherwise they will lose their vibrant colour.

Preheat the oven to 200°C (400°F) gas 6. Grease an ovenproof dish large enough to fit the salmon fillets sitting fairly snugly side by side, but not quite touching. Cover the top of each salmon fillet with a piece of smoked salmon and put into the dish.

Mix together the crème fraîche, Dijon mustard and white wine. You may not need the third tablespoon of white wine. The sauce should be the consistency of double (heavy) cream. Season well with salt and pepper.

Pour over the salmon, and cook in the preheated oven for 15–20 minutes or until the salmon is opaque but still slightly undercooked in the middle – it will continue cooking a little in the residual heat, once out of the oven.

Stir in the snipped chives or roughly chopped dill.

monkfish with fennel, tomatoes and black olives

A very healthy, quick and easy-to-make supper, only taking half an hour from beginning to end. I like to serve this with Slow-fried Lemon and Oregano Potatoes (see page 118).

GET AHEAD

Make to the end of paragraph 2 up to a day ahead, cool, cover and refrigerate. Reheat the sauce and continue with the rest of the method.

HELPFUL HINTS

The tomato sauce may be quite thick before adding the fish but as monkfish has a high water content, don't be tempted to thin it out at this stage.

Serves 4

1 large bulb of fennel or 2 small
1 tbsp olive oil
small knob of butter
salt and freshly ground black pepper
400 g (14 oz) tin (can) of chopped tomatoes
8 anchovy fillets, roughly chopped (optional)

550 g (1¼ lb) monkfish fillets, trimmed of the thin grey membrane and cut into 1-cm (⅛ in) slices
50 g (2 oz) black olives, pitted
1 tbsp basil or parsley, roughly chopped

Remove and discard the outer layer and stalks from the fennel, reserving any green fronds. Peel off any stringy bits with a potato peeler. Halve, quarter and slice quite finely, horizontally.

Heat the olive oil and the butter in a sauté or deep frying pan, add the fennel plus a little salt and cook slowly for about 5 minutes until softened and just beginning to brown. Add the tomatoes (rinse the tin with a little water and add) and anchovies, if using, and bring up to the boil. Check the seasoning, and simmer gently for 5–10 minutes, until the fennel is cooked.

Add the monkfish and black olives and simmer for 5 minutes until the fish is just cooked. Scatter with the reserved fennel fronds and chopped basil or parsley and serve.

Basil in a cold frame

barbecued lobster with lime, garlic and herb butter

The king of shellfish, lobster is not cheap but when bought in season is more reasonably priced. Cheaper (and fresher) still, is to buy it directly from fishermen on the quayside. When buying live lobsters make sure there are rubber bands around the claws as they can be vicious. If only larger lobsters are available buy two and serve half to each person. If barbecuing is not an option, grill the lobsters instead.

Serves 4

*4 live lobsters weighing around 450 g
 (1 lb) each
50 g (2 oz) butter
3 limes*

*2 cloves of garlic, chopped
2 tbsp chopped fresh parsley
salt and freshly ground black pepper*

GET AHEAD
Prepare to the end of paragraph 2 any time on the day you are eating the lobsters, cover and refrigerate.

HINTS AND TIPS
Live lobsters are better cooked the day of purchase. However, they will keep in the fridge overnight if packed in a container with a damp cloth or newspaper around and on top of them. Don't cover with a lid.

When barbecuing make sure the coals are white hot with a thin coating of ash over the top, before cooking. This will take 40–60 minutes after lighting.

Split the lobsters in half from top to bottom by straightening out the tail and inserting the point of a large chopping knife down through the natural cross at the back of the head. It will die instantly. Continue to cut down through the tail and then the rest of the head and split open into two halves. Remove the little sack from the head and the thin black intestine that runs from the head to the tail with the point of a knife. Keep any gooey greenish liver, which is considered a delicacy, and also the roe if there is any, which will be black at this stage.

Put the claws between a cloth and crack with a sharp blow from a rolling pin or hammer. Be careful not to shatter them – just a crack or two.

Melt the butter and add the zest and juice of 1 lime, the garlic, parsley and salt and pepper. Brush the butter over the lobster, put onto the very hot barbecue, cover with a lid if it has one and cook for a few minutes until the lobster shells have turned from black to red and the flesh becomes opaque. Brush with more butter mixture during cooking. If your barbecue has no lid, cook flesh-side down for 2–3 minutes then turn over, brush with more butter and cook until the shells are red and the flesh is opaque. Serve with fresh or charred lime wedges, new, sautéed or Parmentier Potatoes (see page 117) or crusty bread and a large green salad.

quick creamy smoked haddock saffron and chive risotto

This is a bit of a cheat as the stock is added in two stages, needing only sporadic stirring, rather than the classic method which requires hot stock to be added a ladleful at a time with constant stirring. The mascarpone makes it nice and creamy. Do use undyed smoked haddock if you can. It is far superior to the bright yellow version and anyway, the risotto is a lovely bright colour thanks to the saffron.

Serves 4–6

large pinch of saffron strands
2 tbsp olive oil
1 onion, chopped
4 rashers (slices) of smoked pancetta
   or streaky bacon, snipped into strips
2 cloves of garlic, crushed
285–340 g (10–12 oz) smoked haddock,
   diced

400 g (14 oz) risotto rice
150 ml (5 fl oz) white wine
1.2 litres (2 pints) hot chicken stock
salt and freshly ground black pepper
125 g (4½ oz) mascarpone
2 tbsp grated Parmesan cheese
2 tbsp snipped chives

GET AHEAD
Make up to a day ahead to the end of paragraph 4. When cool, cover and set aside. Finish off 15 minutes or so before required. Don't worry about the stock not being hot.

Infuse the saffron strands in 2 tbsp warm water from the kettle. Set aside.

Heat the oil in a large saucepan or wok, add the onion, pancetta or bacon and garlic and cook without browning until the onion is soft.

Add the diced smoked haddock and cook, stirring gently, for about a minute.

Stir in the rice, cook for a few minutes to coat the grains in oil, add the white wine and stir until it has all evaporated. Add the saffron and its lovely yellow liquid, and half the hot stock. Leave to cook for 5–10 minutes or until the stock is absorbed, giving it the odd stir.

Add the rest of the stock and cook for a further 10 minutes. By this time the stock should all be absorbed and the rice just cooked. If the rice still has a bit too much bite, stir in some water and cook until absorbed and the rice is cooked to your liking. The grains should retain a little bite, otherwise, the risotto becomes stodgy.

Check the seasoning and stir in the mascarpone (you may like to add a little more), Parmesan and chives.

sea bass with chorizo and butter beans

A firm favourite we have for supper at least once a week after the fishmonger has been. It takes only minutes to make and is surprisingly filling, so needs little else other than a green salad. Depending on how hungry people are and what else you're eating with it, the butter bean mixture will happily stretch to three people but you will need another sea bass fillet.

'Red Lace' mustard leaf

Serves 2

2 large fillets of sea bass
10 cm (4 in) chorizo, halved lengthways
    and sliced ½ cm (¼ in) thick
8 small cherry tomatoes, halved
pinch of fresh or dried oregano
olive oil
1 clove of garlic, sliced thinly

400 g (14 oz) tin (can) butter beans,
    drained and thoroughly rinsed
salt and freshly ground black pepper
2 large handfuls of baby spinach,
    washed
squeeze of lemon juice
knob of butter

HINTS AND TIPS
A drizzle of lemon oil at the end will enhance most fried fish recipes. Mustard greens, rocket (arugula), Swiss chard or shredded pak choi could replace the spinach.

Slash the skin of the sea bass fillets twice and snip the edge of the skin in one place to help stop it curling up when cooking. Set aside. Warm two plates.

Cook the chorizo in a dry frying pan for a few minutes until its oil begins to run and the chorizo is sizzling. Add the cherry tomatoes and oregano and cook for another few minutes until the tomatoes just begin to soften. Add a little olive oil, followed by the garlic and butter beans and stir until hot. Check the seasoning.

Add the spinach and cook until just wilted. You may need a little more olive oil at this stage. Squeeze over some lemon juice, divide between the two warmed plates and keep warm.

Wipe out the frying pan if necessary, heat a little more olive oil and the knob of butter, season the skin of the sea bass with salt and fry, skin side down first until the skin is brown and crispy; about 2–4 minutes, depending on the thickness of the fillets. Turn over and cook for another minute or two.

Arrange skin side up on top of the butter beans and finish with a good swirl of olive oil over the top.

seafood linguine

A very quick supper or lunch.

Serves 4–6

2 tbsp olive oil
1 small onion, thinly sliced
4 cloves of garlic, finely chopped
1 red chilli (chili pepper), seeded
  and chopped
290 ml (½ pint) passata (strained
  tomato purée)
2 heaped tsp sun-dried tomato paste
pinch of sugar

salt and freshly ground black pepper
400 g (14 oz) frozen mixed seafood
  cocktail (raw is best but cooked is fine)
400 g (14 oz) linguine or spaghetti
handful of chopped fresh parsley
fresh mussels, clams in their shells or
  cooked shell-on prawns (shrimp)
  to garnish, (optional)

GET AHEAD
Make the pasta sauce up to
a day ahead. Leave in the
pan for reheating if using the
same day; otherwise, cool
and store in a bowl in the
fridge, covered.

HINTS AND TIPS
Thin the sauce with a little
pasta water if necessary.

Heat the olive oil in a pan large enough to hold both the pasta and the sauce. Add the onion and cook until soft but not coloured. Add the garlic and chilli and cook for a few more minutes before adding the passata, sun-dried tomato paste, sugar and the frozen seafood. Season well. Bring the sauce up to the boil, stirring occasionally and simmer gently for 5–10 minutes until the fish has thawed out and the prawns have turned pink. If the fish is pre-cooked give it a few minutes less cooking time. Check the seasoning.

Meanwhile, bring a large pan of salted water up to the boil and cook the pasta according to the packet instructions.

If using fresh mussels or clams in their shells, cook them with a splash of water or white wine in a separate pan for a few minutes, until their shells open.

Drain the pasta and gently mix into the sauce with the cooking liquid from the shellfish and chopped parsley. Garnish with the shellfish on top.

monkfish and prawn brochettes with spicy yellow rice

These brochettes on a bed of spicy yellow rice, both look and taste delicious, especially when served with some Foaming Hollandaise Sauce.

Serves 4

550 g (1¼ lb) monkfish fillets
16 raw tiger or king prawns (shrimp), shell on or off
2 tbsp olive oil plus a little extra
juice of 1 lemon
1 red chilli (chili pepper), seeded and finely chopped
7 rashers (slices) of smoked streaky bacon

For the spicy yellow rice
1 tbsp vegetable oil
2 shallots, finely sliced
¼ tsp ground cumin
¼ tsp black mustard seeds
⅛ tsp ground turmeric
⅓ tsp ground coriander
1 clove of garlic, crushed
225 g (8 oz) basmati rice
450 ml (16 fl oz) chicken stock
¼ tsp salt
Foaming Hollandaise Sauce (page 184)

GET AHEAD
Marinate the monkfish several hours in advance, cover and refrigerate. See notes on reheating rice (page 171).

HINTS AND TIPS
If using bamboo skewers, soak them in water for at least half an hour before using to prevent them from burning.

Trim any grey membrane from the monkfish and cut into 20 bite-sized chunks or medallions. Put into a bowl with the prawns, 2 tablespoons of olive oil, the lemon juice and chilli. Leave to marinate for about 30 minutes.

For the rice, heat the oil and fry the shallots for a few minutes, until softened. Add the spices and garlic and stir over the heat for a few more minutes. Add the rice and stir until coated. Add the stock and salt, bring to the boil, stir once and cover with a tight-fitting lid. Leave to barely simmer for 12–15 minutes, until all the liquid has been absorbed. Remove from the heat and leave to stand for a few minutes before removing the lid. Gently stir through with a wooden spoon or fork and either keep warm or serve.

Stretch each rasher of bacon out with the back of a heavy knife and cut into three, vertically. Heat the grill to its highest setting. Wrap a piece of bacon around a piece of monkfish and secure by threading onto a skewer. Follow this with a prawn and then another piece of bacon-wrapped monkfish and so on, until the skewer has five pieces of monkfish and four prawns on it. Repeat this with three more skewers.

Brush with olive oil and grill or barbecue for a few minutes on each side, until the bacon is golden and sizzling. Serve on the rice with the juices spooned over and accompanied with the Foaming Hollandaise Sauce.

salmon en croute with lime and coriander sauce

Lovely pink salmon encased in buttery puff pastry with a bright green, zingy layer in the middle. The delicious sauce has an extra kick from the green chilli (chili pepper).

Serves 8–10

100 g (4 oz) mascarpone
1 tsp fresh ginger, finely chopped
a bunch of spring onions, finely chopped
2 cloves of garlic, crushed
zest of 4 limes
4 tbsp chopped fresh coriander
salt and freshly ground black pepper
500 g (1 lb 2 oz) block of puff pastry
650 g (1½ lb) salmon fillet, skinned

1 egg, beaten with a little salt
sea salt (optional)

For the lime and coriander sauce
500 g (1 lb 2 oz) natural Greek yoghurt
1 green chilli (chili pepper), seeded and finely chopped
juice of 1 lime
1 bunch of fresh coriander
salt and freshly ground black pepper

Preheat the oven to 200°C (400°F) gas 6. Mix the mascarpone, ginger, spring onions, garlic, lime zest and coriander together and season well with salt and pepper.

Cut the puff pastry in half and roll out each half just enough to be able to cut out two large circles, using a dinner plate as a template (about 27 cm/10½ in). The second circle should be very slightly larger than the first.

Put the smaller pastry circle onto a baking sheet lined with silicone paper. Lightly score a rim 2 cm (¾ in) from the edge being careful not to cut all the way through the pastry. Brush the rim with the beaten egg avoiding the cut edges.

Slice the salmon across into chunky strips, about 2 cm (¾ in) thick, and place over the middle of the pastry, avoiding the rim and stacking it up a little in the middle. Spread the mascarpone mixture over the top. Lay the second pastry circle over the top, press the edges together and crimp using a thumb and index fingers. Lightly score a diamond pattern over the top of the pastry. Decorate with leaves made from the pastry trimmings if you like.

Brush with beaten egg, avoiding the cut edges, sprinkle over a little sea salt and cook for 15–20 minutes until puffed up and golden brown.

Mix the yoghurt, chilli and lime juice together. Twist the fat lower stalks from the coriander and discard. Chop the remainder and stir into the yoghurt. For a runnier sauce add a little cold water. This will depend on the yoghurt you use.

baked vietnamese sea bass

An incredibly quick, fresh and tasty supper or lunch adapted from a recipe I learnt during a recent trip to Vietnam. Good with jasmine rice and pak choi.

Mint

Serves 4

For the sea bass
vegetable oil
200 g (7 oz) shiitake mushrooms, sliced
salt and freshly ground black pepper
4 sea bass fillets
6 spring onions, trimmed and thinly sliced lengthways
2.5 cm (1 in) piece fresh ginger, peeled and cut into thin batons
1 red chilli (chili pepper), halved, seeded and thinly sliced horizontally

handful of fresh coriander, roughly chopped
handful of fresh mint, roughly chopped

For the sauce
2 tbsp oyster sauce
1 tbsp soy sauce
1 tbsp fish sauce (nam pla)
½ tbsp sesame oil
juice of 1 lime

GET AHEAD
Cook the mushrooms, prepare the spring onion, ginger and chilli topping and make the sauce up to a day in advance. Keep covered, separately, in the fridge.

HINTS AND TIPS
Other white fish fillets could be used such as haddock, cod or sea bream. Oyster mushrooms could be used instead of shiitake.

Preheat the oven to 190°C (375°F) gas 5.

Heat 1 tbsp of oil in a frying pan, add the mushrooms, season with salt and pepper and cook until dry and beginning to brown.

Lay the sea bass fillets in a shallow ovenproof dish, greased with a little oil. Mix together the mushrooms, spring onions, ginger and chilli. Scatter over the fish fillets.

Using the same bowl mix all the sauce ingredients together and spoon over the fish. Cook in the oven for 10–15 minutes or until the fish is opaque and just cooked. Scatter the chopped coriander and mint over the top just before serving.

cheesy haddock, prawn (shrimp) and spinach gratin

A contemporary and effortless take on the classic Haddock Mornay. I often use crème fraîche, mustard and cheese instead of a roux-based cheese sauce; easier, lighter and just as good. Perfect for a quick supper but also for a supper party, as being completely prepared in advance all you have to do is pop it in the oven and perhaps cook a few new potatoes.

Serves 4

450 g (1 lb) spinach, washed
salt and freshly ground black pepper
300 g (10½ oz) raw, peeled tiger or king
   prawns (shrimp) (frozen weight),
   thawed
110 g (4 oz) Gruyère cheese, grated

1 heaped tsp Dijon mustard
5 tbsp crème fraîche
good handful of fresh dill, thick stalks
   removed and fronds chopped
450 g (1 lb) haddock, cod or coley
   fillets, skinned

GET AHEAD
Make the sauce and cook the spinach the day before, cover and refrigerate individually. On the day, prepare up to the baking stage several hours in advance, cover and keep in the fridge.

HINTS AND TIPS
Smoked haddock would be a tasty alternative. I like to use peeled raw prawns with the tail shells left on as they look attractive.

Preheat the oven to 220°C (425°F) gas 7.

Cook the spinach, in the water left clinging to the leaves after washing, with 1 tsp salt until just wilted. Drain and squeeze out all the liquid with your hands. Spread over the bottom of a *shallow* greased ovenproof dish just large enough to fit the fish in one layer.

Drain the prawns and spread onto paper towel to drain further until needed.

Mix together the cheese, mustard, crème fraîche and dill and dot half of this mixture over the spinach. Don't worry; there will be gaps between the dots but when cooked they will melt into a delicious sauce. Lay the fish fillets, cut into manageable sized pieces on top, nestle the prawns in and around and season. Dot over the rest of the cheese mixture.

Bake for 15 minutes until bubbling and beginning to brown just around the edges.

meat

Cuts of meat range vastly in price so there is something to suit most pockets. Cheaper cuts tend to need a longer cooking time but often have much more flavour. This is reflected in the recipes in this chapter, some of which call for leftovers, which I always think is a bit of a derogatory term and rather off-putting for something that can be so delicious. Think of using up leftovers as the beginning of a recipe rather than the end.

côte de boeuf with green peppercorn sauce

Côte de Bôeuf is a classic restaurant dish, usually 'pour deux personnes', requiring you to find a friend with whom to share this special treat. Often served on a chopping board and accompanied by béarnaise sauce it is one of life's great pleasures. My take on this classic dish is excellent for entertaining as everything can be prepared in advance.

Serves 4–5

1 rib of beef (900 g–1.2 kg/2–2 lb 10 oz),
   chined and French trimmed
   (see Butcher's Notes)
olive oil
salt and freshly ground black pepper

a splash of red wine or water
1–2 tsp Dijon mustard
4–5 tbsp crème fraîche
2 tsp green peppercorns

Preheat the oven to 220°C (425°F) gas 7.

Weigh the rib in order to calculate the cooking time. Smear with a little olive oil and season both sides and the edges with salt and pepper.

Heat a frying pan until very hot and sear the meat for 2–3 minutes each side or until caramelised to a good brown colour. Brown the sides as well. Transfer to a small non-stick shallow roasting tin or baking sheet.

Cook according to the times opposite. Remove from the oven and transfer to a plate to rest somewhere warm for at least 15 minutes.

While the beef is cooking, pour off most of the fat from the frying pan, put back onto the heat, add a little water or red wine and scrape all the caramelised cooking juices off the bottom. Stir in the mustard, crème fraîche and green peppercorns plus a little of their juice. Bring up to the boil and simmer for a few minutes. Check the seasoning. You may like to add a little more crème fraîche. Set aside.

Slice the beef on the diagonal, add any meat juices from the plate or board to the sauce, reheat, tip into a warmed jug and serve.

GET AHEAD
Brown the meat and make the sauce up to a day ahead. Cool, cover and refrigerate seperately. Cook and reheat when required.

HINTS AND TIPS
If cooking more than one rib, brown separately but transfer to a single tin or baking sheet and roast together. Add 5 minutes to the cooking time. Salsa Verde (page 185) or Foaming Hollandaise (page 184) would be delicious alternative sauces.

BUTCHER'S NOTES
Ask your butcher for well-hung beef – ideally it should be hung for at least three weeks.

Well-hung beef isn't always kept on display largely because the flesh is dark and the fat is a deep creamy colour which looks less appealing to the shopper than bright red meat and white fat. So ask if there is any well-hung meat available.

Chined and French trimmed is the classic way racks of lamb are prepared.

COOKING TIMES
These are based on cooking the meat immediately after browning, while it is still warm. If cooking from room temperature, add an extra 5 minutes.

900 g (2 lb) = 10 minutes
1–1.2 kg (2 lb 4 oz–1 lb 10 oz) = 15–18 minutes
Anything over the above weights = 20 minutes

braised steaks with mustard and capers

This only takes a few minutes to prepare despite the long cooking time so you can put it in the oven and forget about it. An easy, tasty and inexpensive supper.

Serves 4

*4 x 140–175 g (5–6 oz) slices of braising
  steak such as topside (round steak)*
seasoned flour
olive oil
1 onion, thinly sliced
large pinch of dried oregano
150 ml (5 fl oz) red wine

4 tsp Dijon mustard
3 tsp capers, plus a little of their juice
200 ml (7 fl oz) beef stock
salt and freshly ground black pepper
*crème fraîche and chopped fresh
  parsley, to garnish (optional)*

Preheat the oven to 180°C (350°F) gas 4. Snip through the fat and membrane of the steaks (this stops them curling up when browning) and coat each one lightly in the seasoned flour.

Heat a little oil in a sauté pan and brown the steaks well on both sides. (You may need to do this in batches depending on the size of your pan, as the steaks will stew and will not brown if the pan is overcrowded). Remove from the pan. Add more oil if necessary, then add the onion and oregano and cook until beginning to soften and brown. Pour in the red wine and bubble fast for 1 minute. Add the mustard, capers, plus some of their juice and the stock or water.

Bring to the boil, check the seasoning, return the meat to the pan or transfer everything to an ovenproof serving dish, cover with a lid or foil and cook for 1 ½ hours. Swirl in some crème fraîche and chopped parsley just before serving, if you like.

GET AHEAD
Cook several days in advance, cool, cover and keep in the fridge, or freeze. Reheat at 190°C (375°F) gas 5 for 20–25 minutes or until piping hot.

HINTS AND TIPS
For a more elegant presentation arrange the steaks overlapping down the middle of an oval platter or dish and spoon over the sauce.

beef or lamb harissa rissoles with tomato sauce

As a way of using leftover beef or lamb, rissoles make a welcome change from shepherd's pie, delicious though it is. They do need to be highly seasoned. A salsa (see page 185) would be a nice sharp alternative to the tomato sauce.

Serves 4

450 g (1 lb) cooked beef or lamb,
  minced
1 small onion, very finely chopped
2 cloves of garlic, crushed
1 tbsp harissa paste
50 g (2 oz) fresh breadcrumbs
1 tsp salt
freshly ground black pepper
2 eggs, beaten
olive oil, for frying
natural Greek yoghurt and fresh
  coriander to serve

For the tomato sauce
a glug of olive oil
250 ml (9 fl oz) passata (strained tomato
  purée)plus 100 ml (4 fl oz) water
1 tbsp sun-dried tomato purée
large pinch of dried oregano
salt and freshly ground black pepper
½ tsp sugar

GET AHEAD
Make the rissoles, cover and chill up to 2 days in advance. The sauce will keep in the fridge for 2–3 days.

HINTS AND TIPS
If time is short, serve with sweet chilli (chili pepper) sauce instead of tomato sauce.

Put all the tomato sauce ingredients into a saucepan, bring up to the boil and simmer for 5–10 minutes.

In a large bowl, mix the first eight ingredients together well. This is best done with your hands. Be generous with the black pepper and taste to make sure the mixture is well seasoned. Divide roughly into eight and shape into rounds in your hands.

Heat a thin layer of olive oil in a frying pan, add the rissoles, press down a little with a fish slice, and fry until golden brown. Turn over, lower the heat and cook slowly for a further 10 minutes or until heated all the way through and well browned. You may need to do this in two batches depending on the size of your frying pan.

Serve with the tomato sauce, a dollop of Greek yoghurt and some roughly chopped coriander on top of each rissole.

roast fillet (tenderloin) of beef with mixed mushrooms, french (green) beans, red onion and roast garlic

This is dinner party fare for special occasions. Devised to be prepared ahead, there are several components but they can all be cooked in stages and well in advance. It looks magnificent with everything served on one or two platters, leaving little to do at the last minute, your guests impressed and you relaxed. Serve with Crispy Straw Potato Galettes (page 116) or Parmentier Potatoes (page 117).

PREPARING THE BEEF
I like to tie up a fillet before roasting as it produces a long narrow barrel shape the same thickness all the way along, which in turn cooks more evenly and gives perfectly shaped round slices when carving. Often a fillet is thicker in some places than others but tied up this way, as if by magic, it becomes a uniform size. Tie a piece of thin household string around the middle of the fillet, knot and trim the ends. Then, moving out along each side from the middle, repeat at roughly 4 cm (1½ in) intervals.

Serves 6

For the beef and vegetables
3 bulbs of garlic
olive oil
salt and freshly ground black pepper
30 g (1 oz) butter
225 g (8 oz) fresh wild or shiitake mushrooms, large ones sliced
225 g (8 oz) oyster mushrooms, large ones sliced (or a mixture of any mushrooms such as button and chestnut)
a little lemon juice
1 tbsp olive oil
1 large or 2 small red onions, sliced
2 tsp balsamic vinegar

400 g (14 oz) extra-fine French (green) beans, topped but not tailed
1.2 kg (2½ lb) whole middle-cut fillet (tenderloin) of beef, trimmed and tied (see Preparing the Beef, right)

For the sauce
1 heaped tsp Dijon mustard
290 ml (½ pint) beef stock
1 tbsp Worcestershire sauce
1 tsp tomato purée
50 ml (2 fl oz) red wine
50 ml (2 fl oz) Madeira, Marsala or brandy
a little butter (optional)

Prepare Ahead
Everything in this section can be prepared up to a day in advance, cooled, covered and kept in the fridge. If using on the same day, leave at room temperature, until reheating.
    Preheat the oven to 200°C (400°F) gas 6.

Slice the pointed tops off the bulbs of garlic and place on a large piece of foil. Pour over a little olive oil, sprinkle with some salt and draw the foil up to form a loose parcel. Put on a baking sheet and bake for 50 minutes or until soft and tender. When cool enough to handle, break or snip the heads into halves or quarters. Set aside.

Melt the butter in a frying pan and cook the mushrooms with a squeeze of lemon juice and a little salt until all the liquid has evaporated and they are starting to brown. Set aside in the pan.

Heat 1 tbsp of olive oil in a saucepan and cook the onion with a pinch of salt until soft. Add the balsamic vinegar and continue to cook, stirring occasionally until very soft and caramelised. Add to the mushrooms.

Meanwhile, put all the sauce ingredients, except the butter, into a saucepan, whisk together, bring up to the boil and simmer fast until reduced by half, about 15–20 minutes. Taste and season if necessary, although if using a stock (bouillon) cube it probably won't need it.

Cook the beans in boiling salted water, drain and cool completely under cold water. Spread onto paper towel and roll up. Set aside.

Season the prepared fillet generously with salt and pepper, and sear very well in a little very hot fat in a frying pan, until a good dark colour all over, including the ends. Remove from the pan, cool and cover.

Cooking the beef

The following steps can be started 45 minutes–1 hour 15 minutes (depending on resting time) before you are planning to serve the beef.

Preheat the oven to 220°C (425°F) gas 7. Heat a little fat in an ovenproof frying pan or roasting tin just big enough to hold the fillet, add the fillet and when sizzling well transfer to the top of the oven. Cook for 15 minutes. Remove from the tin onto a cold plate, leave to sit for a few minutes to stop the cooking process, then put somewhere warm to rest for a minimum of 30 minutes. (1 hour is fine and even better.) Pour off the fat, put the roasting tin over the heat and deglaze with a little water, scraping off all the caramelised juices. Add to the sauce.

Just before serving, toss the beans and garlic with a little olive oil over a high heat, in a saucepan or wok, for a few minutes until hot. Reheat the mushroom mixture and add to the beans.

Reheat the sauce. Add any juices from the beef to the sauce and whisk in 2–3 knobs of butter if using (this enriches the sauce and makes it shiny). Pour into a warmed jug.

Remove the string from the beef, carve and arrange the slices overlapping around the edge of a warmed platter. Pile the vegetables into the middle and scatter over the garlic. Serve with the sauce.

roast rump of lamb with creamed flageolet beans and redcurrant sauce

A lovely small boneless joint of very tender lamb cut from the top of the leg. Ideal for entertaining, as it has a short cooking time and is easy to carve.

Pea pods

Serves 4

*1 large whole lamb rump or chump
  (see notes opposite)*
soy sauce
olive oil
2 tbsp redcurrant jelly
2 tbsp red wine vinegar
290 ml (½ pint) chicken stock
1 onion, chopped finely
1 small sprig of rosemary, leaves

chopped or a pinch of dried
1 clove of garlic, crushed
*1 x 400 g (14 oz) tin (can) of flageolet
  beans, drained and well rinsed*
*2 tbsp double (heavy) cream or
  crème fraîche*
*a good handful of petit pois (peas),
  cooked salt and freshly ground
  black pepper*

GET AHEAD
Prepare everything to the end of paragraph 3 up to a day ahead, cool, cover and chill.

HINTS AND TIPS
Cooked fine French (green) beans can be added to the flageolet beans as well as, or instead of, the peas. Try not to stir the beans too much as they will break up and become mushy.

NOTES ON BUYING AND COOKING RUMP OF LAMB
Rumps, or double chumps, of lamb vary in weight, depending on the size of the lamb, which depends on the time of year. An average rump weighs between 540–700 g (1 lb 3 oz– 1 lb 9 oz).

Anything below the above weights should only take 15 minutes with the same resting period.

Marinate the lamb rump in a splash of soy sauce and olive oil. Leave overnight or for as long as possible. This is not vital – an hour or two is better than nothing.

In a small saucepan heat the redcurrant jelly and vinegar with the stock. Bring to the boil and simmer until reduced by about half.

Meanwhile, fry the onion in a little olive oil until soft. Add the rosemary and garlic and cook for another minute. Add the flageolet beans, season and heat through. Set aside.

Preheat the oven to 220°C (425°F) gas 7. Drain the lamb from the marinade, season the skin with a little salt and freshly ground black pepper and roast for 15–20 minutes for pink lamb. The cooking time will depend on the weight of the rumps. (see opposite.) The meat should give slightly when prodded with your finger. When cooked, leave the lamb to rest for at least 20 minutes.

Reheat the sauce and the beans, adding the cream and peas to the beans just before serving. Serve the lamb thinly sliced and arranged on top of or around the beans either on one platter or individual plates. Spoon over a little of the redcurrant sauce if you like and serve the rest in a jug.

stuffed marrow (squash)

I was brought up on marrow (squash) and still absolutely love it. Instead of the usual way of stuffing it lengthways, I prefer cutting into rounds, which looks more appealing and is easier to serve. The quick toppings turn the whole thing into a lovely bubbling and irresistible gratin.

Serves 3–4

1 tbsp olive oil
1 onion, chopped
1 clove of garlic, crushed
a pinch of dried oregano
450 g (1 lb) minced lean lamb or beef
2 tsp tomato purée
1 tsp Dijon mustard
1 tbsp flour
150 ml (¼ pint) water
salt and freshly ground black pepper
1 marrow (squash), roughly
  1.3–1.8 kg (3–4 lbs)

Topping 1
2 tbsp crème fraîche
2 tbsp grated Parmesan cheese
  (see page 176)

Topping 2
2 tbsp breadcrumbs (see page 176),
fresh
  or dried
2 tbsp grated Cheddar cheese

Heat the oil in a saucepan, add the onion, garlic and oregano and cook until soft. Add the lamb or beef and cook, stirring, until it has all taken on some colour. Add the tomato purée, mustard, flour, water and seasoning and bring up to the boil, stirring all the time. Simmer for 5–10 minutes until thickened a little. Check the seasoning. It should be well seasoned.

Preheat the oven to 200°C (400°F) gas 6. Cut the marrow into rings about 5 cm (2 in) deep. Peel the rings and remove the seeds from the centre. Arrange in a greased, shallow, ovenproof dish into which they fit snugly.

Season lightly and fill the marrow rings with the mince. Drizzle over a little olive oil and cook for 45 minutes–1 hour or until the marrow is soft and cooked through, depending on the size and age of the marrow.

Mix together the ingredients for your chosen topping and spoon over each ring. Return to the oven for another 10 minutes until golden brown and bubbling. You may need to raise the oven temperature for speedier browning.

GET AHEAD
Prepare up to a day in advance until the end of paragraph 2. Cover the marrow and filling separately and keep in the fridge. Both toppings can be made up to 2 days in advance, covered and chilled.

Stuff the marrow several hours in advance.

HINTS AND TIPS
This is a good way of using up leftover cooked lamb or beef. Mince the meat briefly in a processor, being careful not to overdo it.

Leave the skin on the marrow if you like, but if it is a bit on the old side, it will be tough however long you cook it. It also turns a rather unattractive colour.

butterflied moroccan lamb with couscous

One of the easiest, tastiest and best ways I know for feeding a crowd. Economical too, as a large boned leg of lamb stretches easily to feed up to 12 people. The couscous is fresh and zingy with the addition of preserved lemons and fresh herbs. I also like to serve this with a cucumber raita, as it makes a cool contrast to the highly spiced lamb.

GET AHEAD
Marinade the lamb 24–36 hours ahead.
   Make the couscous up to a day in advance but omit the herbs until just before serving. If serving the couscous warm, reheat it in a shallow, ovenproof dish in a medium oven for 10 minutes or until warm.

Serves 8–12, depending on the size of leg

*1 large leg of lamb, butterfly boned (ask
   the butcher to do this)
salt and freshly ground black pepper*

For the marinade
*1 x 90 g jar of harissa paste
3 cloves of garlic, crushed
2 tsp ground cumin
1 tsp ground coriander
1 tbsp vegetable oil
2 tsp salt
2 tbsp lemon juice*

For the couscous
*500 g (1 lb 2 oz) couscous
large pinch of ground cumin
570 ml (1 pint) boiling chicken stock
2 tbsp olive oil
6–8 small preserved lemons, less if large
2 large handfuls of pine nuts, toasted
bunch of fresh mint, chopped
bunch of fresh coriander or parsley (or
   both) leaves chopped
Cucumber Raita (see page 177) and
   warm flatbreads, to serve*

HINTS AND TIPS
The lamb is also delicious when barbecued. Make sure the coals are white-hot (40–60 minutes from lighting) and use the same oven timings.
   If eating outside, the lamb is delicious stuffed into the pockets of individual naan or pitta breads with a good dollop of Cucumber Raita and some couscous as well if you like.

Mix all the marinade ingredients together. Weigh the lamb to calculate the cooking time, put it into a large bowl and smear the marinade over both sides, massaging it into all the nooks and crannies. Fold the wings of the lamb back over into the middle, put skin side down in the bowl, cover and leave to marinate at room temperature for an hour or so and then in the fridge for at least 24 hours.

   Preheat the oven to 240°C (475°F) gas 8. Lift the lamb out of the bowl, and spread out, skin side up, in a shallow roasting tin. (Scrape some of the marinade off the skin if you prefer a less charred effect when cooked.)

   Sprinkle some fine salt over the skin and roast at the top of the hot oven for about 30 minutes (see Cooking Times, right). The lamb should be pink all the way through and will feel fairly springy when prodded with a finger. Too rare and your finger will

COOKING TIMES
1.5–1.8 kg (3½–4 lb) = 20 minutes

2.25 kg (5 lb) = 25–30 minutes

2.7 kg (6 lb) = 30–35 minutes

slow-braised pork belly with puy lentils and salsa verde

Three of my very favourite things and all together! Chinese greens make a lovely accompaniment if you would like more than just lentils.

Serves 4

1.3 kg (2 lb 4 oz) belly pork, individually boned and scored vertically
4 cloves of garlic, unpeeled and halved, plus 1 finely chopped
2 onions, 1 quartered and 1 finely chopped
4 star anise

100 ml (3½ fl oz) soy sauce
olive oil
2 sticks of celery, stringy bits removed and finely diced
250 g (9 oz) Puy lentils
salt and freshly ground black pepper
Salsa Verde (see page 185)

GET AHEAD
Prepare to the end of paragraph 1 up to 3 days ahead. Reheat the pork in the liquid when required or see alternative serving instructions.

Prepare to the end of paragraph 2 up to 2 days ahead. Reheat the lentils in a saucepan with a little extra olive oil for a few minutes.

HINTS AND TIPS
Salt toughens lentils so season after cooking.

Put the pork into a lidded casserole, which it fits snugly. Add the garlic, the quartered onion, star anise and soy sauce. Pour in enough water to barely cover the pork – 300–425ml (½–¾ pint). Bring up to the boil, cover with a disc of greaseproof paper and the lid and simmer very gently for 2 hours. Or simmer for 5 minutes and transfer to an oven preheated to 170°C (325°F) gas 3 for the same length of time. Leave in the liquid until needed.

Heat 1 tbsp olive oil in a saucepan and fry the chopped onion, garlic and celery for a few minutes until soft. Add the lentils and stir to coat in the oil. Add 600 ml (1 pint) water, bring up to the boil and simmer for 15–20 minutes or until soft but still with some bite. Drain and rinse until the water runs clear. Return to the pan and season with salt and freshly ground black pepper.

Stir a little olive oil into the lentils, heat through and spoon onto a serving platter, shallow dish or individual plates. Take the pork from its liquid, remove the skin, carve into chunky slices and arrange on top of the lentils. Moisten with a spoonful or two of the liquid and serve with a slick of Salsa Verde over the top and the rest separately.

For an alternative way of reheating the pork, place the whole joint in the top of a very hot oven on a rack or bed of scrunched-up foil for about 15 minutes. The skin may not be crispy but it will be brown, soft, gelatinous, tasty and meltingly tender.

roast belly of pork

Succulent, melting, slow-roast belly of pork is hard to beat. It is one of the cheapest cuts of meat, which, due to its high fat content and long, slow cooking, remains succulent. I always serve this with Raspberry Vinegar (page 178). The sweet sour flavour is the perfect piquant foil to the richness of the pork.

Serves 8

2.3–2.7 kg (5–6 lb) whole pork belly boned and trim, skin very finely scored (see Butcher's Notes, opposite)
salt and freshly ground black pepper

1–2 tbsp plain (all-purpose)flour
Raspberry Vinegar (see page 178), to serve (optional)

Place the pork in the sink and pour a kettle of boiling water over the skin. Dry on paper towel. This helps to create crispy crackling.

Select a roasting tin long enough to take the pork comfortably. Using a very large piece of foil, make a rough sausage-shaped mound roughly the same length as the pork. Put this in the roasting tin and gently lie the pork on top. The pork should be sitting on the foil in a rounded arc shape, with no dips and troughs in the skin. Re-mould the foil a little to achieve this if necessary. Moisture will accumulate in any sunken parts during cooking, thus preventing the skin from crackling.

Massage a good teaspoon of fine salt into the skin and leave uncovered in the fridge for several days (24 hours minimum).

Preheat the oven 220°C (425°F) gas 7. Remove the pork from the fridge for at least an hour before cooking. Rub with a little more salt and cook at the top of the hot oven for 20–30 minutes, or until the skin is nicely crackled. Reduce the oven to 170°C (325°F) gas 3 and cook slowly for 1½ hours until the pork is meltingly tender. Remove from the tin and leave to rest for at least 20 minutes.

To make a slightly thickened gravy, drain any juices from the foil back into the tin. Skim off most of the fat. Remove any odd burnt bits. Stir a tablespoon or so of flour into the fat and juices, then gradually add 600 ml (1 pt) stock or water, stirring all the time to prevent lumps. Bring up to the boil, check the seasoning and pour into a jug. For a thin gravy, omit the flour, scrape off all the goody bits and bubble until syrupy.

Put some Raspberry Vinegar on the table in a pretty jug or glass bottle so your guests can pour a little over their pork.

HINTS AND TIPS
If the crackling needs crisping up in places at the end of the cooking time (which occasionally it does), give it a burst at the top of a hot oven or under the grill.

BUTCHER'S NOTES
Ask your butcher for a whole pork belly, individually boned. He will take each rib bone out individually, leaving behind as much meat as possible (important as meat is quite scarce on this cut). Secondly, ask him to score the skin very finely, vertically along the joint. If you can, buy the belly several days before you need it, thus giving the skin time to dry out in the fridge, which in turn produces really crispy crackling.

pork loin steaks with seedy mustard, apple and sage

Purple sage

This takes less than half an hour from beginning to eating! Just the job for a last-minute supper.

Serves 4

4 x 140 g (5 oz) pork loin steaks
  (some supermarkets sell thinner steaks,
  in which case you will need 8)
1 tbsp olive oil
a small knob of butter
salt and freshly ground black pepper
4–5 large sage leaves, chopped
150 ml (¼ pint) apple juice or cider

1 tbsp seedy mustard
5 tbsp crème fraîche
4 spring onions trimmed and thinly
  sliced (optional)

GET AHEAD
Make up to 2 days in advance, cool, cover and chill but don't add the spring onions, if using, until after reheating.

HINTS AND TIPS
Chicken stock and 1 tbsp of honey can be substituted for the apple juice or cider. Savoy or sweetheart cabbage, thinly shredded and steamed or stir-fried until just wilted, is the perfect accompaniment

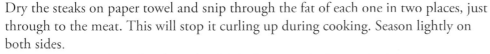

Dry the steaks on paper towel and snip through the fat of each one in two places, just through to the meat. This will stop it curling up during cooking. Season lightly on both sides.

In a sauté pan heat the olive oil, add the butter and when melted fry the steaks for a few minutes on each side, until turning golden brown. Remove onto a plate.

Add the sage to the pan with the apple juice or cider and bubble up, scraping all the goody bits off the bottom. Stir in the mustard and crème fraîche and when bubbling, return the steaks and any juices. Cover with a lid or foil and simmer very gently for 8–10 minutes. As soon as the pork feels firm when prodded, it is done. Scatter with the spring onions just before serving, if using.

lamb's liver schnitzel

The secret of these delicious schnitzels is very thinly sliced liver. I have served this many times with mashed or sautéed potatoes and a tomato and finely chopped red onion salad. Nowadays, I lean towards Salsa Verde, wilted spinach and new potatoes or the Tomato, Shallot and Parsley Salsa (page 185). Delicious either way.

Serves 6

550 g (1¼ lb) lamb's liver, whole if possible (or, sliced very thinly, diagonally, no thicker than 2–3 mm (¹⁄₁₆–⅛ in) slices by the butcher)
flour for coating, seasoned with salt
2 eggs lightly beaten with a pinch of salt

110 g (4 oz) fine dried breadcrumbs (see page 176)
olive oil
a knob or two of butter
1 lemon

GET AHEAD
Coat the liver slices in breadcrumbs up to two days in advance, cover and chill or freeze.

If slicing the liver yourself, peel off the very fine membrane that coats the entire surface and snip out any other bits that you don't like the look of. With a sharp knife (I use a carving knife) carefully slice into the thinnest possible slices – no thicker than 3 mm (⅛ in). You should have around 12 slices.

Spread some seasoned flour, the beaten eggs and the breadcrumbs onto three separate dinner plates. Working with three or four slices of liver at a time, coat them firstly in the flour, then the egg and finally the breadcrumbs, shaking off any excess crumbs. Place on a tray or plate large enough to hold the liver roughly in one layer or stack up between layers of clingfilm.

Heat the oil and a little butter in a frying pan. When the butter is frothing add the first batch of liver. Fry for a few minutes until golden brown and crispy and then turn over for a minute or two to brown the other side. Remove to a warm serving plate and keep warm whilst cooking the rest. You may need to add a little more oil and butter between each batch. Serve overlapping down the platter with the lemon wedges and Salsa Verde or Tomato, Shallot and Parsley Salsa (page 185).

poultry

In this chapter you will find recipes suitable for both family meals and entertaining, some plain and some with richer sauces which chicken lends itself to so well. The better the quality of life poultry has had, the better the texture and flavour will be when it's cooked.

duck breasts with peas and mint

A favourite family supper which can be produced in no time at all. Excellent for entertaining as well, as everything can be prepared in advance with very little to do at the last minute. New potatoes are the only accompaniment needed.

Serves 4

4 duck breasts (about 170 g/6 oz each), trimmed
salt and freshly ground black pepper
a knob of butter
1 bunch of spring onions, trimmed and thinly sliced

450 g (1 lb) frozen peas (petit pois) or fresh peas
pinch of sugar
150 ml (¼ pint) double (heavy) cream or crème fraîche
a handful of mint leaves, chopped

Broad beans, peas, carrots and courgettes

Preheat the oven to 220°C (450°F) gas 7. Score the skin of the duck breasts in a diamond pattern using a sharp knife. Rub the skin with salt.

Heat a dry frying or sauté pan, add the duck breasts skin side down and cook for a few minutes until the skin is deep golden brown. Turn over and cook for a further minute or two just until the underside is sealed. Remove the breasts onto a baking sheet or shallow roasting tin, skin side up.

Cook for 6 minutes in the preheated oven.

Meanwhile pour off all but 1 tablespoon of fat from the frying pan, add the butter and spring onions and cook slowly until beginning to soften. Add the peas, season with salt, pepper and a pinch of sugar and cook until thawed, if frozen or tender if fresh, stirring occasionally. Add the cream or crème fraîche, bring up to the boil and bubble for a few minutes until thickened a little. Stir in the chopped mint.

Allow the duck to rest for six minutes in a warm place before slicing diagonally and serving on top of the peas with any juices from the duck poured over.

GET AHEAD

Sear the duck breasts (without putting them in the oven) and prepare the peas up to a day in advance. Cool, cover and chill if not eating the same day, otherwise set aside until required. Don't add the mint to the peas until just before serving.

HINTS AND TIPS

If reheating the peas, you may need to thin out with a little extra cream, crème fraîche or water. Tarragon could be substituted for the mint and chicken stock for the double cream or crème fraîche.

COOKING AND RESTING

A fairly reliable guide for cooking duck breasts is to allow 1 minute per 25 g (1 oz). So a 170 g (6 oz) sealed breast will need 6 minutes in the oven, if cooking immediately after sealing, and 6 minutes resting. If cooking a sealed breast from cold, add an extra 2 minutes to the cooking time. These timings should produce pink meat.

baked parmesan chicken with tomato and fennel penne

A rustic, tasty 'all-in-one dish' perfect for lunch or supper. Serve with a bowl of crisp green salad.

Serves 4–5

2 tbsp olive oil
1 onion, chopped
2 bulbs of fennel, trimmed, quartered
   and cut into chunks
2 cloves of garlic, crushed
large pinch of dried oregano or thyme

1 x 400 g (14 oz) tin (can)
   chopped tomatoes
a pinch of sugar
salt and freshly ground black pepper
225 g (8 oz) penne pasta
8 chicken thighs, trimmed
Parmesan cheese, grated (page 176)

GET AHEAD
Prepare the sauce and pasta, mix together and put into the ovenproof dish up to a day ahead.

Lemon and golden thyme

Heat the oil in a saucepan, add the onion, fennel, garlic and oregano or thyme and cook slowly, stirring occasionally, until beginning to soften around the edges. Add the tomatoes plus half a can of water, a pinch of sugar and season well. Bring to the boil and simmer for 10–15 minutes. Check the seasoning.

Preheat the oven to 200°C (400°F) gas 6. Bring a pan of salted water to the boil and cook the penne according to the packet instructions. Drain and add to the tomato and fennel sauce. Tip into a greased shallow ovenproof dish.

Arrange the chicken thighs on top of the penne, season, scatter generously with grated Parmesan cheese and a little olive oil.

Cook for 45–60 minutes until crisp and golden and the chicken is cooked through.

chicken breast with parma ham, goats' cheese and pesto sauce

This is nice and easy and looks impressive. Serve with small pasta shapes or potatoes and some spinach or French (green) beans. I often serve this cold too and as such it is excellent for picnics or summer buffets.

Serves 4

olive oil
4 small, skinless, boneless chicken
  breasts, trimmed
8 slices of Parma ham
a few young spinach leaves, washed
  (optional)

1 x 100 g (3½ oz) small round creamy
  goats' cheese, cut into four
125 ml (4 fl oz) white wine
200 ml (7 fl oz) crème fraîche
2 tbsp pesto sauce (or seedy mustard)

Preheat the oven to 220°C (425°F) gas 7. Lightly grease a shallow roasting tin, just large enough to fit the chicken breasts comfortably.

Slice a pocket into each breast horizontally, being careful not to cut all the way through. Line with two or three spinach leaves, if using, and stuff with a piece of goats' cheese. Reshape the chicken breast so that the stuffing is completely enclosed.

Place 2 slices of Parma ham slightly overlapping on a chopping board (forming a square-ish shape) and place a chicken breast cut side up at one end of the ham. Roll the ham up around the breast making a tight oblong parcel with all but the ends of the breast concealed. Put into the roasting tin seam side down to secure the parcel and repeat with the rest.

Drizzle a little olive oil over the top and cook for 10–12 minutes depending on the size of the breasts. Remove from the roasting tin and keep warm. It matters not if some of the cheese has oozed out.

Add the wine to the roasting tin and reduce by half over a high heat, scraping the cheesy cooking sediment from the bottom of the tin. Stir in the crème fraîche (you might not need it all) and any juices from the chicken. Add the pesto (or mustard), check the seasoning and pour into a warmed jug.

Slice the chicken either into rounds or cut each breast in half diagonally to reveal the lovely oozing stuffing.

GET AHEAD
Prepare the chicken breasts before cooking up to a day in advance, cover and refrigerate. If eating cold, cook the chicken breasts up to a day in advance, cool, cover and refrigerate. Slice straight from the fridge as early as you like on the day and cover.

HINTS AND TIPS
Served cold, this looks very pretty sliced into rounds and arranged overlapping in concentric circles on a large platter. Sun-dried or sun blush tomatoes added to the stuffing gives lovely extra colour, especially if the spinach is included too.

Serve with a bowl of mayonnaise let down to your desired consistency, and perhaps a little dribbled over the chicken. Mix with some Greek yoghurt for a lighter sauce or for a lovely vivid green sauce, blitz together with a good handful of fresh basil leaves.

vietnamese herby chicken with nutty green rice salad

Vietnamese food is defined by the freshness of its ingredients and as a result is light, healthy and very flavoursome. Marinated chicken crops up on menus throughout Vietnam. This dish is very easy to make and delicious accompanied by the verdant nutty rice salad that can be served hot or cold.

Serves 4

For the chicken

1 tbsp coriander seeds
1 tsp chopped ginger
1 tsp salt
freshly ground black pepper
4 cloves of garlic, roughly chopped
vegetable oil
handful of fresh mint leaves, chopped
handful of fresh coriander, chopped
zest and juice of 2 limes
8 chicken thighs, trimmed of fat and any excess skin

For the rice

225 g (8 oz) mixed basmati and wild rice
450 ml (16 fl oz) chicken stock
salt and freshly ground black pepper
4 spring onions, chopped
2 sticks of celery, stringy bits removed and diced
handful of cashew nuts, toasted and roughly chopped
handful of pine nuts, toasted
handful each of fresh coriander, mint and parsley leaves
olive oil
natural yoghurt, to serve

GET AHEAD

Marinate the chicken up to a day in advance. Cook the rice up to a day in advance and stir in the vegetables and nuts. Cool, cover and keep in the fridge. Add the finely chopped herbs just before serving. If serving hot follow instructions for reheating rice (page 177).

HINTS AND TIPS

This allows for two chicken thighs per person. To extend to six people use another three or four thighs but there is no need to up the marinade. The rice will happily feed six as well.

Using a small grinder, processor or pestle and mortar make a paste with the coriander seeds, ginger, 1 tsp salt, pepper and garlic. Add 1 tbsp vegetable oil and process or pound again. If using a processor, tip the paste into a small bowl and then stir in the mint, coriander and lime zest and juice.

Slash each chicken thigh twice right through the skin and into the meat. I use scissors for this. Put the thighs into a bowl or plastic bag and smear all over with the marinade. Refrigerate overnight, turning once if you remember.

Remove the chicken from the fridge at least an hour before cooking. Preheat the oven to 220°C (425°F) gas 7.

Spread the thighs out in a roasting tin or ovenproof dish, skin side up, reserving the remaining marinade. Scatter some salt over the top and cook for 35 minutes until golden brown and charred in places.

Check the chicken after 25 minutes and if browning too fast, either reduce the temperature or cover loosely with a piece of foil for the final 10 minutes. If not browning, pour off the liquid into the reserved marinade and return to the oven for the final 10 minutes. Remove from the tin and keep warm.

Meanwhile, put the rice into a saucepan with the stock and ½ tsp salt. Bring up to the boil, stir, cover and simmer very gently for 15–20 minutes or until all the liquid has been absorbed.

Put the spring onions, celery, cashews and pine nuts into a mixing bowl, add the rice and mix everything together well.

Chop the herbs finely – I like to do this in a herb chopper as when chopped this way they turn the rice vivid green – add to the rice and mix well. Moisten with a little olive oil. Finally, check the seasoning – it should be very flavoursome.

Remove any badly charred bits from the roasting tin and skim off any fat. Add the reserved marinade to the cooking juices and a little extra water. Bring up to the boil, scraping the bits off the bottom and bubble for 2–3 minutes. Check the seasoning, pour into a jug and serve with the chicken, nutty green rice and a bowl of natural yoghurt.

all-in-one pot roast chicken and vegetables

I just love pot roasts—chicken in particular. This is one of my all-time favourites. It couldn't be easier, a virtually no effort, all-in-one casserole that is succulent, wholesome and plain, and is open to infinite variations. If you are in the mood for something a little more enriched, stir in a swirl of double (heavy) cream or crème fraîche at the end, or serve with Salsa Verde (see page 185).

Broad beans

Serves 4

1 x 1.5 kg (3 lb 5 oz) chicken, at room
  temperature
salt and freshly ground black pepper
olive oil
knob of butter
500 g (1 lb 2 oz) small new potatoes, or
  larger ones halved
8 shallots,
1 head of garlic, cloves peeled

2 sprigs fresh thyme or tarragon, or a
  large pinch of dried
150 ml (5 fl oz) white wine or water
3 good handfuls of peas or broad (fava)
  beans, or a mixture of both, fresh or
  frozen (optional)
cream or crème fraîche (optional)
chopped parsley or mint

GET AHEAD
Prepare to the end of paragraph 1 any time during the day of eating.

HINTS AND TIPS
You can skip browning the chicken. Smear it with butter and season, then cook and remove the pale skin before serving.

Preheat the oven to 200°C (400°F) gas 6. Untruss the chicken, remove any lumps of fat from just inside the cavity and season well all over. Heat a little olive oil and butter in a large, heavy casserole and brown the chicken all over, turning it carefully so you don't break the skin. Nestle the potatoes, shallots, garlic and herbs around the chicken.

Season the vegetables, pour the wine or water around the edge and bring up to a good rolling boil. Put on the lid and cook in the oven for 1 hour.

Remove the chicken, potatoes and shallots from the casserole and keep warm in a shallow serving dish. Skim off some of the fat if you like and add the peas and/or broad beans, if using. Bubble up the juices for a few minutes to cook the vegetables and enrich with cream or crème fraîche, if using. Stir in the chopped parsley or mint. Spoon the delicious vegetables and juices around the chicken. If you find it easier, carve the chicken separately and arrange on top of the vegetables tipping in any escaped juices. The chicken may fall apart easily which is just what it's meant to do.

fricassee of chicken and wild mushrooms

Intense, rich, creamy and velvety– these are just some of the reasons to choose this delicious fricassée for entertaining. The fact that it can be made well in advance and frozen just adds to its appeal.

Serves 4

25 g (1 oz) dried wild mushrooms
a little olive oil
85 g (3 oz) butter (you may not
* need it all)*
8 chicken thighs, trimmed
4 shallots, thinly sliced

150 ml (5 fl oz) white wine
290 ml (10 fl oz) chicken stock
290 ml (10 fl oz) double (heavy) cream
* or crème fraîche*
salt and freshly ground black pepper
parsley to garnish, optional

Snip or snap the larger mushrooms into smaller pieces, put into a small bowl and soak in enough warm water just to cover. Leave for at least 30 minutes.

Heat 1 tablespoon of oil and 55 g (2 oz) of the butter in a sauté pan. Season the skin of the chicken and cook, skin side down, very gently for 25 minutes. Season, then turn over and cook for a further 10 minutes or so, until cooked through. Remove from the pan and skim off most of the fat leaving 1–2 tablespoons. If the fat is at all burnt, pour it all away and wipe out the pan with paper towel.

If necessary, melt the remaining 30 g (1 oz) butter and add the shallots to the pan. Strain the mushrooms, reserving the liquid and add to the shallots. Cook gently for 5 minutes, then turn up the heat and add the wine, letting it bubble for 2 minutes before adding the stock and mushroom liquid, leaving the dregs behind in the bottom of the bowl. Bring to the boil and reduce by half. Add the cream or crème fraîche and simmer for a minute or two until you have a slightly thickened, luscious, velvety sauce.

Return the chicken, skin side up, bubble for a few minutes until heated through and check the seasoning.

GET AHEAD
Make up to two days in advance, cool, cover and refrigerate or freeze. If serving with basmati and wild rice, see notes on cooking rice in advance (see page 177).

HINTS AND TIPS
Either leave in the sauté pan for reheating or (to save last-minute washing up) arrange in an ovenproof serving dish and reheat, covered, in a medium oven for 25–30 minutes until hot and bubbling.

griddled chicken with oyster mushrooms and coriander

The flavour of this is much bigger than the sum of its parts. It is very fresh and incredibly healthy, as all things griddled tend to be. Add a few new potatoes and you have a lovely quick lunch or supper.

Serves 2

3 tbsp olive oil
125 g (4½ oz) oyster mushrooms
salt and freshly ground black pepper
juice of 1 lime
1 clove of garlic, crushed
1 small red chilli (chili pepper),
  seeded and finely sliced

2 spring onions, trimmed and finely
  sliced lengthways
2 chicken breasts, trimmed if necessary
a handful of fresh coriander leaves,
  roughly chopped

Fry the mushrooms in 1 tbsp oil with a little salt and pepper until all the liquid has evaporated and they are beginning to turn golden brown. Set aside.

In a mixing bowl, combine the rest of the olive oil, the lime juice, garlic, chilli, and spring onions and season with salt and pepper.

With a rolling pin or the bottom of a saucepan flatten out the chicken breasts between two large sheets of clingfilm to roughly 5 mm (¼ in) thick. Heat a dry griddle (or frying) pan until very hot. Rub the chicken breasts with olive oil and salt and griddle, flattening with a fish slice until they are golden brown and lift easily off the pan. This will only take a few minutes. Flip over and repeat, although this side will only take a minute to cook.

Add the warm mushrooms and coriander to the dressing, stir well, spoon over the chicken breasts and serve.

GET AHEAD
Prepare the mushrooms, chilli, spring onions and chicken up to a day in advance, cover and chill individually. Don't combine everything until required.

HINTS AND TIPS
When griddling, heat the griddle until very hot and then a little hotter still. Always rub the oil into the food, never the griddle. The first side always takes longer than the second and if the food isn't ready to turn it will resist and leave fibres stuck to the pan. When ready it will easily lift straight off.

rosemary chicken with french (green) bean, fennel, sun-blush tomato and feta salad

Delicious warm or cold, this can easily be expanded to feed a crowd, and makes a good outdoor feast if you barbecue the chicken. See page 84 for notes on griddling.

Serves 4

4 chicken breasts
olive oil
juice of 1 lemon (2 tbsp)
2 sprigs of rosemary, leaves chopped
1 small bulb of fennel
½ red onion, thinly sliced

100 g (4 oz) sun-blush or sun-dried
   tomatoes
100 g (4 oz) feta cheese, diced
450 g (1 lb) small new potatoes
350 g (12 oz) French (green) beans
salt and freshly ground black pepper
1 tbsp red wine vinegar

GET AHEAD
Marinate the chicken and cook the potatoes and beans several hours in advance. Reheat the vegetables, if serving warm, just before required.

HINTS AND TIPS
Look for 'feta cheese' on the packet rather than 'Greek or feta style' cheese as these are not the real McCoy. Obviously a lovely slice of fresh feta is best of all.

Bash out the chicken breasts between 2 sheets of clingfilm using a rolling pin or the bottom of a saucepan, to roughly 5 mm (¼ in) thick. Put them into a bowl with a little olive oil, the lemon juice and rosemary and leave to marinate until you are ready to cook them.

Remove and discard the outer layer and stalks from the fennel, reserving any green fronds from the top, cut in half and finely slice lengthways. Combine the fennel, onion, tomatoes and feta cheese in a large mixing bowl with 2 tablespoons of olive oil.

Cook the new potatoes and French beans separately until just tender. Drain and keep warm.

Heat a dry griddle (or frying) pan until very hot. Season the chicken breasts and griddle for a few minutes on each side, until just cooked. Arrange on a platter.

Add the potatoes and beans to the salad, season with salt, pepper, some olive oil and the red wine vinegar and then heap over the top of the griddled chicken. Scatter over the fennel fronds if you remember, which I rarely do!

slow-cooked Chinese duck legs

This is quick to prepare with a long, slow cooking time and a deep, warming flavour. Serve with creamy mashed potatoes or egg noodles and something green such as pak choi, cabbage or spinach.

Serves 4

4 duck legs, trimmed of any excess fat
1 tsp Chinese five spice powder
150 ml (¼ pint) water
2 tbsp soy sauce
2 tbsp dry sherry
1 tbsp sweet chilli (chili pepper) sauce

1 tbsp honey
1 tsp fresh ginger, peeled and
 finely chopped
2 cloves of garlic, peeled and chopped
2 star anise

GET AHEAD
Make up to 2 days in advance (which benefits the flavour), cover and refrigerate or freeze. Skim the fat from the top and reheat until bubbling.

Pre-heat the oven to 180°C (350°F) gas 4.

Rub the duck legs with the five spice powder. Heat a dry saute pan or shallow ovenproof casserole, add the legs skin side down, brown very well, turn over and brown the other side. Remove from the pan and pour off the excess fat.

Put the pan back onto the heat and add the water, scraping off any sediment from the bottom. Add the rest of the ingredients, mix together well then return the legs to the pan with any juices. Most of the skin should be exposed. Bring up to the boil, cover and cook in the oven for 1½ hours.

Alternatively simmer very gently for the same length of time. The skin won't be super-crisp but it won't be soggy either and will taste delicious. However, for crispy skin turn the oven up to 220°C (425°F) gas 7, remove the lid and crisp up for 10-15 minutes. Skim the excess fat off the top if you like and serve.

weekend lunches

Most of the recipes in this chapter are one-dish wonders – something prepared and ready just to shove into the oven or dress up when required, with all the preparation and washing up out of the way. You will find recipes for all weathers, different times of the year, for varying numbers, some to be served hot and some cold. Almost everything is what I call 'dig-in food' – put it on the table and let everyone help themselves.

tartiflette

A delicious rib-sticking rustic dish from the French Alps.
Reblochon is the local cheese traditionally used, however
Tallegio or Fontina make excellent alternatives.

Serves 4–6

1 kg (2 lb 4 oz) waxy new potatoes such
*   as Charlotte, unpeeled*
olive oil
knob of butter
1 onion, finely sliced
200 g (7 oz) of smoked bacon, snipped
*   into chunks (or smoked lardons)*

2 cloves of garlic, crushed
200 g (7 oz) Reblochon, Taleggio or
*   Fontina cheese, sliced with rind on*
salt and freshly ground black pepper
284 ml (½ pint) double (heavy) cream
*   or crème fraîche*

GET AHEAD
Prepare to the end of
paragraph 4 up to 24 hours
in advance. Cool, cover and
refrigerate until required.

Preheat the oven to 200°C (400°F) gas 6.

Cook the potatoes in boiling salted water until just tender. Drain and when cool
enough to handle, cut into two or three thick slices, lengthways.

Whilst the potatoes are cooking, heat the olive oil and butter in a frying pan and
cook the onion gently until it begins to soften. Add the bacon or lardons and garlic
and continue cooking until the mixture is soft and beginning to brown.

Grease a shallow ovenproof dish and layer with half each of the potatoes, the onion
and bacon mixture and cheese respectively. Season and repeat with the rest.

Pour the cream, or dot the crème fraîche over the top and bake for 10–15 minutes
or until golden brown and bubbling.

italian meatballs with tomato sauce

These slightly spicy meatballs are perfect for a weekend lunch and delicious enough for a supper party, possibly preceded by a platter of antipasti as a starter, thus leaving only the pasta to cook at the last minute.

Serves 4–5

450 g (1 lb) shoulder of lamb, minced
3 sprigs of fresh oregano or a large pinch of dried
3 tbsp grated Parmesan cheese (see page 176)
2 tbsp breadcrumbs (see page 176)
2 tbsp parsley, chopped
½ tsp chilli (chili pepper) powder
1 egg, beaten
1 tsp salt

freshly ground black pepper and nutmeg
1 tbsp olive oil
1 x 400 g (14 oz) tin (can) of chopped tomatoes
pinch of caster (superfine granulated) sugar
basil or parsley to decorate
350 g (12 oz) papparadelle or tagliatelle to serve

Put the lamb, oregano, Parmesan, breadcrumbs, parsley, chilli powder, egg, salt, pepper and nutmeg into a bowl and mix together very well – hands are best! Wet your hands and mould into small balls about the size of a golf ball. Put on a plate and chill for at least half an hour to allow them to firm up.

Heat the olive oil in a sauté pan that has a lid and fry the meatballs until golden brown on all sides. Spoon off the excess fat if there is too much. Add the chopped tomatoes and sugar, season with salt and pepper and carefully turn the meatballs to coat them in the sauce. Bring to the boil, cover (use foil if your pan doesn't have a lid) and simmer gently for 15–20 minutes until the tomatoes have formed a thickish sauce. Turn them once or twice during the cooking time. Thin with a little water if necessary.

Serve with paparadelle, tagliatelle or spaghetti, cooked according to the packet instructions and tossed with a splash of olive oil. Either pile the meatballs and sauce on top of the pasta on a platter, scattered with basil or parsley, or serve separately.

GET AHEAD
Make and cook the meatballs and sauce up to 2 days in advance, cool, cover and refrigerate or freeze.

ANTIPASTI SUGGESTIONS
A selection of the following would make a delicious and stunning-looking starter arranged on a large platter; Parma ham, Bresaola, marinated olives in little pots, salamis, mortadella, buffalo mozzarella, caper berries, roast artichoke hearts in oil, chargrilled red (bell) peppers, small chunks of salty Pecorino cheese, quartered fresh figs, marinated anchovies, Focaccia or other Italian breads and dipping bowls of good olive oil.

pasticcio

The beauty of this is that the sauce and bits and bobs take the same amount of time to prepare as the pasta takes to cook. So it's a real quickie that can be prepared entirely in advance.

Basil

Serves 5–6

2 tbsp olive oil
1 x 400 g (14 oz) tin (can) of chopped
  tomatoes
2 cloves of garlic, crushed
a sprig of fresh thyme, or a pinch
  of dried
salt and freshly ground black pepper
a pinch of sugar
350 g (12 oz) penne pasta
300 g (10½ oz) mascarpone cheese
6 anchovies, roughly chopped

8 slices of Parma ham
handful of basil leaves
200 g (7 oz) Taleggio cheese, thinly
  sliced
olive oil

GET AHEAD
Make up to a day ahead, cool, cover and refrigerate. If cooking from cold, it might need a little longer in the oven.

Preheat the oven to 200°C (400°F) gas 6. Put a large pan of salted water on to boil for the penne. Meanwhile, heat the olive oil in a small saucepan and add the tomatoes, garlic, thyme, seasoning and sugar. Bring to the boil and simmer the sauce very gently until the pasta is ready.

Cook the penne according to the packet instructions. Drain and return to the saucepan. Add the mascarpone and anchovies, stirring, until the mascarpone has melted. Add the tomato sauce and check the seasoning.

Tip half of the pasta into a greased ovenproof dish. Tear half the Parma ham into largish strips and lay on top of the pasta nestling them in a little. Tear the basil leaves and scatter over, followed by half the Taleggio cheese. Top with the rest of the pasta and the last of the Taleggio. Tear the remaining Parma ham into strips and nestle in scrunched up waves between the cheese.

Swirl with a little olive oil and cook for 20 minutes or until golden brown and bubbling hot.

slow-roast shoulder of lamb boulangère

Perfect for a weekend lunch, especially if you have a busy morning with little time to spend in the kitchen. Pop the lamb and potatoes in the oven in one dish and forget about it for three hours or more. The longer it's cooked, the softer the meat becomes and will just fall off the bone.

Serves 6–8

2.7–3.2 kg (6–7 lb) shoulder of lamb, on the bone, (knuckle left on)
5 cloves of garlic, quartered lengthways
5 anchovies
2 sprigs fresh rosemary
1.3 kg (3 lb) floury (baking) potatoes, eg.. Maris Piper

2 onions
large knob of butter, softened
290 ml (½ pint) hot lamb or chicken stock or water
salt and freshly ground black pepper
Mint Sauce (see page 178) and redcurrant jelly, to serve

Preheat the oven to 200°C (400°F) gas 6. Butter a roasting tin or baking dish large enough for the lamb to sit happily on top of the potatoes, which should come up to about 2.5 cm (1 in) below the rim. Trim the lamb of any excess fat and with a small knife, stab it on both sides at random intervals and stuff the holes with bits of garlic, roughly torn anchovy and sprigs of rosemary.

Cut the potatoes into thin discs. (The easiest way of doing this is by using the slicing disc of a food processor, or a mandolin.) Cut the onions in half and slice them thinly in the same way. Mix the potatoes and onions together with the chopped leaves from a sprig of rosemary and season with ½ tsp salt and some black pepper.

Tip the potato mixture into the buttered dish or roasting tin, level it out evenly and place the lamb on top, pushing down a little to nestle it into the potatoes. Smear the lamb with the softened butter and season with salt and freshly ground black pepper.

Pour the hot stock or water into the dish and cook for 3 hours. If after the first two hours or so the lamb and top layer of potatoes are deep golden brown and crispy, turn the oven down to 190°C (375°F) gas 5 and loosely lie a sheet of foil over the top for the rest of the cooking time.

Carve the lamb into thick slices and serve with the potatoes, Mint Sauce and redcurrant jelly.

GET AHEAD
Prepare the lamb with the garlic, anchovies and rosemary up to a day ahead. Cover and keep in the fridge. Bring back to room temperature at least an hour before cooking.

HINTS AND TIPS
The cooked lamb will keep for up to an hour somewhere warm. Delicious with Creamed Spinach (see page 122), a plain green vegetable or a large bowl of salad.

my version of zuni chicken and bread salad

Oh, I just love this. Irresistible, delectable and delicious! My humble version of world-renowned chef Judy Rodgers' (of the Zuni Café in San Francisco) famous Zuni Chicken recipe. People flock from all over the world to her restaurant and in particular for the chicken and bread salad. I would not presume to adapt her recipe to improve on it, merely to offer a simplified version for the home cook. As her recipe wisely advises, make extra bread or you won't have enough left by the time the chicken is ready to eat!

Once you have tried this method of salting a chicken for several days before cooking, you will never roast one in the usual way again. It is easy, but you do have to think a few days ahead. Salting produces very tender, succulent, juicy, perfectly seasoned chicken. Try it and see!

Serves 4–5

1 x 1.4–1.6 kg (3¼–3½ lb) chicken, untrussed
4 good sprigs of thyme, rosemary, marjoram or sage
salt and freshly ground black pepper
1 loaf of ciabatta or other country bread, a day-old
olive oil
1 tbsp currants

red wine vinegar
3 tbsp white wine vinegar
1 bunch of spring onions, trimmed and sliced diagonally
3 cloves of garlic, slivered
2 tbsp pine nuts, toasted
a few handfuls of mixed salad leaves

Salt the chicken 2–3 days before required. Stuff the herbs inside the bird. Measure ½ tsp sea salt per pound of chicken and rub well all over the chicken, distributing more over thicker parts. Cover and leave in the fridge for 2–3 days.

The bread salad can be prepared up to several hours in advance. Preheat the oven to 200°C (400°F) gas 6. Tear the bread into irregular chunks – some will be bite-sized, some bigger, some just fat crumbs. Toss with a little olive oil and sea salt and cook for 6–8 minutes on a baking sheet, until brown and crispy. Tip into a large bowl. When ready to cook the chicken, turn the oven on to 220°C (425°F) gas 7.

Put the currants into a ramekin and just cover with red wine vinegar. Set aside.

Whisk together the white wine vinegar, 8 tbsp of olive oil and salt and pepper to taste and toss 3 tablespoons over the bread. Some bits will be dressed, some won't.

Fry the spring onions and garlic gently in a little olive oil for a few minutes until just softened, stirring all the time. Tip over the bread if using immediately. If not, set aside until the chicken is cooking. Drain the plumped up currants, reserving the vinegar, and add to the bread along with the pine nuts.

Put a roasting tin, into which the chicken fits snugly, into the preheated oven. Rinse the chicken and dry very well. Put into the hot roasting tin (it should sizzle) and cook for 50–60 minutes, depending on the size of the chicken. Remove from the tin and leave to rest.

Skim most of the fat from the juices in the roasting tin, then put over the heat and when sizzling add a little water and scrape off the sediment. Reduce a little and add to the bread.

Toss some more of the dressing over the bread. Taste and add seasoning and possibly some reserved vinegar, if necessary. Joint the chicken into eight or cut up the joints and slice the breasts into chunky bits.

Arrange the bread on a large platter mixing in the salad leaves, nestle the chicken in over the top and spoon over any juices.

Variegated salad leaf

sausage, apple and onion lattice pie with salsa

A simple weekend dish that is very good for picnics too. It is much easier than it looks. The better the quality of the sausages the better the pie, so buy the best you can afford – spicy or herby perhaps – and remove them from their skins.

Serves 4–6

1 tbsp olive oil
1 onion, finely chopped
1 large cooking apple (such as Bramley), peeled, cored and cut into small chunks
2 cloves of garlic, crushed
1 tbsp fresh sage, chopped
salt and freshly ground black pepper
450 g (1 lb) sausages, slit, skins peeled off and removed

1 tbsp tomato purée
1 tbsp English mustard
1 tsp Worcestershire sauce
375 g (13 oz) ready rolled puff pastry
1 egg, beaten with a little salt
Tomato, Shallot and Parsley Salsa (see page 185)

GET AHEAD
Make in advance to the end of paragraph 2 up to a day ahead, cover and refrigerate, or freeze. Thaw before cooking and glazing with egg.

Heat the oil in a frying pan and cook the onion until beginning to soften. Add the apple, garlic and sage and continue to cook until soft and amalgamated but retaining a few chunky bits of apple. Season and tip into a large mixing bowl. Allow to cool a little. Add the sausage meat, tomato purée, mustard and Worcestershire sauce and mix together well. Hands are best for this. Allow to cool completely.

Preheat the oven to 200°C (400°F) gas 6. Unroll the pastry and release from but leave it on its wrapping. Pile the sausage meat down the middle of the longest length leaving a 2.5 cm (1 in) border at either end. Brush the margins of the pastry with the beaten egg, bring the short ends up over the sausage meat and brush their tops with egg. Bring the long sides up and over to enclose the sausage meat, sealing the seams well. Using the wrapping as an aid, turn over onto a baking sheet (lined with silicone paper, if you have it) so that the seam is underneath.

Brush well all over with beaten egg and, using a sharp knife, slash a chevron (upside down V) pattern down the top of the pastry, about 1 cm (½ in) apart. Don't worry if you cut through in places. Cook for 20 minutes until a rich golden brown, then turn the oven down to 180°C (350°F) gas 4 for a further 15 minutes. If it is browning too fast, put a piece of foil loosely over the top. Serve hot, warm or cold with the Tomato, Shallot and Parsley Salsa.

chicken and mushroom gougère

Guaranteed to excite both the taste buds and the eyes! Don't be alarmed at the rather wet sticky raw choux – it rises as if by magic into an airy puff of cheesy deliciousness.

Serves 4–6

50 g (2 oz) butter
1 onion, chopped
175 g (6 oz) chestnut mushrooms, sliced
large pinch of dried oregano or tarragon
450 g (1 lb) chicken thighs or breasts,
  cut into strips (approx 3 breasts)
2 tbsp plain (all-purpose) flour
1 tbsp Dijon mustard
4 tbsp dry sherry (optional)
290 ml (½ pint) chicken stock
salt and freshly ground black pepper
4 tbsp crème fraîche

a handful of fresh parsley, chopped
2 tbsp dried breadcrumbs
  (see page 176)

For the choux pastry

110 g (4 oz) plain (all-purpose) flour
pinch of salt, pepper and cayenne
85 g (3 oz) butter
220 ml (7½ fl oz) water
3 eggs, lightly beaten
50 g (2 oz) Gruyère or strong Cheddar
  cheese, cut into ½ cm (¼ in) cubes

GET AHEAD
Make the chicken and mushroom filling up to two days in advance, cool, cover and refrigerate.
  Prepare choux pastry before adding the eggs, several hours in advance and leave in a food processor, or covered in a bowl, until you are ready to continue with the next step.

HINTS AND TIPS
The gougère will wait happily somewhere warm for half an hour or so after cooking.
  Pheasant and Celery or Smoked Haddock and Leeks are alternative filling ideas. Ham or bacon could also be added to any of them and for vegetarians a mushroom filling with celery or bell peppers would be good.

Preheat the oven to 200°C (400°F) gas 6. Melt the butter in a deep sauté pan. Add the onion, cook until soft, then add the mushrooms and herbs and cook until beginning to brown around the edges. Add the chicken, cook until starting to brown, then add the flour, mustard, sherry and stock. Bring to the boil and simmer for a few minutes until the mixture has thickened. Stir in the crème fraîche, check the seasoning, pour into a bowl and leave to cool. Overnight is best. Stir in the parsley.

For the pastry, mix the flour, salt, pepper and cayenne together in a bowl. Heat the water and butter in a large saucepan. When the butter has melted, bring it to a rolling boil, add the flour, take off the heat and beat with a wooden spoon until the mixture leaves the sides of the pan having formed a stiff, smooth dough. Transfer to either a mixing bowl or a food processor.

Gradually beat the eggs into the pastry mixture until the choux has a dropping consistency. You may not need it all. This is most easily done in a processor. Stir in the diced cheese. Spoon the mixture around the edge of a shallow ovenproof dish (roughly 37 x 23 cm (14½ x 9 in)). Pile the chicken mixture into the centre, making sure you leave the pastry uncovered, sprinkle the filling with the crumbs and bake until the choux is well risen and golden – about 50–60 minutes.

bubble and squeak cakes with smoked haddock, fried eggs and bacon

Just the job for a weekend brunch, possibly accompanied by a large jug of spicy Bloody Mary, complete with crunchy celery sticks. An excellent way of using up leftover vegetables too.

Serves 4

175 g (6 oz) cooked sprouts, cabbage or peas
350–450 g (12–16 oz) mashed potato
salt and freshly ground black pepper
flour for coating
4 undyed smoked haddock fillets, about 115–175 g (4–6 oz) each

8 rashers (slices) of pancetta or streaky bacon
olive oil and butter for frying
4 eggs
a few chives (optional)

GET AHEAD
Make up to two days in advance to the end of frying the pancetta, then, cool, cover everything individually and refrigerate.

HINTS AND TIPS
The potato and sprout quantities are approximate and only a guide. This is all about leftovers, so just use whatever you have and your imagination.

Chop or mash the vegetables with the back of a fork. Stir into the potato and season (it should be well seasoned). Shape into four cakes and coat each with a little flour.

Put the smoked haddock fillets into a sauté or frying pan, barely cover with water and bring very slowly up to the boil. If using two large fillets, cut them in half first. Remove from the heat immediately. Set aside.

Fry the pancetta or bacon until crispy, drain on paper towel and set aside.

Add a little butter to the bacon fat and some extra olive oil if necessary and fry the cakes slowly on a low heat, carefully turning once, until they are golden brown on both sides and heated through.

When ready to serve, fry the eggs. Whilst they are frying, drain the haddock fillets and sit one on top of each cake, followed by the eggs and then finally a crisscross of pancetta or bacon. You might like to snip over some chives and a grinding of black or cayenne pepper too.

raised pork pie

In my experience, most people think they aren't up to making a raised pie and are amazed when they see just how easy it is. A pie never fails to impress, is perfect for any time of the year and is, I think, easier than a tart, which requires baking blind. Hot water crust pastry is easy to make and mould with your hands. That combined with some raw pork in the middle is all there is to it.

Serves 10–12

450 g (1 lb) pork shoulder or leg
450 g (1 lb) boneless, rindless belly
  pork
225 g (½ lb) gammon (uncooked ham)
2 tsp chopped fresh sage
1 tsp ground coriander
1 tsp ground allspice
2 tsp anchovy essence
1½ tsp salt
freshly ground black pepper

For the pastry

450 g (1lb) plain (all-purpose) flour
1 tsp salt
200 g (7 oz) lard
30 g (1 oz) butter
225 ml (8 fl oz) milk and water, mixed
  (125 ml / 4 fl oz of each)
1 beaten egg, to glaze

GET AHEAD
The pie will last for up to a week in the fridge.

HINTS AND TIPS
I don't add jelly to my pies at the end as they have plenty of their own. However, if you would like to, add a softened leaf or two of gelatine to a small amount of good stock and pour it through a funnel, inserted into the top of the pie, whilst it is still warm. A tin (can) of consommé is a good (cheat's!) alternative to stock.

Preheat the oven to 190°C (375°F) gas 5. Roughly cut all the meat into no bigger than 5 mm (¼ in) pieces or ask your butcher (very nicely!) to do this for you. This can be done in a processor but be careful not to over-process. Put into a bowl and add the rest of the ingredients, mix well and set aside.

For the pastry, mix the flour and salt together. Bring the lard, butter, milk and water to the boil in a large saucepan. Remove from the heat and immediately add the flour, stirring quickly until a malleable dough has formed. When cool enough to handle, cut off a quarter of the dough for the lid. Wrap in clingfilm and keep warm.

Place the rest of the warm dough in a spring-form tin measuring 20 cm (8 in) across and 6–8 cm (2½–3in) deep. Work the pastry along the bottom and up the sides until it is just above the top of the tin. Try to get it evenly distributed, especially in the 'corners' at the bottom where it tends to bulk up. Fill with the pork mixture and brush the slightly overlapping pastry at the top with egg glaze.

Roll the reserved pastry into a circle, between two sheets of clingfilm for easy transportation, to make a lid. Lay it on top of the pie, pressing the edges together well.

Cut off any excess pastry and crimp the edges together. Cut a small cross in the centre and press a small plain metal piping nozzle into the hole. Decorate the pie with pastry trimmings and glaze with the beaten egg.

Cook on a baking sheet for 30 minutes. Turn the oven down to160°C (325°F) gas 3 and cook for a further 1½ hours. Cover loosely with foil if the pie starts to become too brown. Leave to cool in the tin. Cover and refrigerate overnight or until needed.

chicken, fennel and potato tray bake

Nice and effortless for the weekend. Just put the roasting tin on the table and let everyone dig in.

Serves 4

1 kg (2¼ lb) waxy salad potatoes such as Charlotte
2 cloves of garlic, thinly sliced
2 bulbs of fennel

2 tbsp balsamic vinegar
salt and freshly ground black pepper
olive oil
8 large chicken thighs, trimmed

Preheat the oven to 220°C (425°F) gas 7. Grease a large shallow roasting tin big enough to fit the chicken thighs in one layer fairly spaciously and to fit all the potatoes snugly, but not layered too deeply.

Cut the potatoes lengthways, into three or four slices and tip into the greased roasting tin. Scatter over the garlic and season with a little salt and pepper and a good glug of olive oil. Give the dish a good shake to level out the potatoes.

Remove and discard the outer layers and stalks from the fennel, reserving any green fronds. Slice finely and scatter over the top of the potatoes. Spoon over the balsamic vinegar.

Rub the skin of the chicken thighs with a little salt and pepper and arrange on top of the fennel.

Cook for 45 minutes to 1 hour or until the chicken is golden brown and crispy and the potatoes feel soft and tender when stabbed with a knife. Scatter over the chopped fennel fronds.

spicy sausage, lamb and bean bake

A satisfying, warming all-in-one dish, this is a sort of sausage version of cassoulet. Jacket (baked) potatoes are a good accompaniment—they turn this into a very substantial and sustaining meal. Crusty bread and a salad would be a less filling alternative.

Serves 6

olive oil
6 sausages (spicy Italian are good)
280–350 g (10–12 oz) lamb neck fillet, trimmed and cut into chunky slices
1 large onion, halved and each half cut into 8 segments
a large pinch of dried oregano
2 cloves of garlic, chopped
1 tsp harissa paste
1 tbsp English mustard

2 x 400 g (14 oz) tins (cans) of chopped tomatoes
pinch of sugar
2 x 400 g (14 oz) tins (cans) of haricot (navy) beans (or 1 tin [can] of haricot [navy] beans and 1 tin [can] of cannellini beans), drained and rinsed
salt and freshly ground black pepper
85g (3 oz) fresh breadcrumbs, (see page 176)
fresh parsley, chopped (optional)

GET AHEAD
Prepare up to a day in advance (before adding the breadcrumbs), cool, cover and refrigerate. Allow a slightly longer cooking time if it is being cooked from cold. Alternatively make entirely in advance up to 2 days ahead, cool, cover and refrigerate or freeze and reheat when required.

HINTS AND TIPS
Thin with a little water if you like a runnier sauce. Toulouse sausages or cooking chorizo would also be delicious.

Preheat the oven to 200°C (400°F) gas 6.

Heat a little olive oil in a sauté pan and cook the sausages until nicely golden brown all over. Put into an ovenproof dish and cut or snip each one into three chunks. Brown the lamb, adding a little more oil if necessary and add to the sausages. Add the onion to the pan, again adding a little more oil if necessary and when softened a little, add the oregano and garlic and cook for another minute or so. Add the harissa paste, mustard, tomatoes, sugar and finally the beans to the pan, stirring together well. Bring up to the boil and check the seasoning. Tip the mixture over the sausages and lamb.

Sprinkle with the breadcrumbs and cook in the preheated oven for 50–60 minutes, until golden brown and bubbling. Check that the top isn't browning too fast and if necessary cover very loosely with foil for the last part of the cooking time. If using, scatter the parsley over the top just before serving.

spanakopita

This classic Greek pie can be cut up into small pieces and served with drinks, perhaps instead of a starter, and is excellent for picnics, being very portable in or out of its dish. Or, just be traditional and serve warm with a tomato and onion salad. A slice or two of Serrano ham and a big bowl of crispy green leaves would also be good.

Serves 8

200 g (7 oz) cooked spinach
  (500 g / 1 lb 2 oz fresh weight)
225 g (8 oz) feta cheese
salt and freshly ground pepper

nutmeg
3 eggs
70 g (2½ oz) butter, melted
1 packet of filo pastry

GET AHEAD
Make up to 2 days ahead, cool, cover and refrigerate. Warm in a moderate oven when required or serve cold.

Preheat the oven to 190°C (375°F) gas 5. Squeeze as much water as possible out of the spinach and chop roughly. Put into a bowl, crumble in the feta and season with salt, pepper and a little nutmeg. Add the eggs, beating them together a little at the side of the bowl, before stirring into the mixture.

Melt the butter and use a little to brush well all over a 24 cm (9½ in) loose-bottomed tart tin or ovenproof dish.

Unroll the filo pastry, remove a sheet and cover the rest with a damp cloth to prevent it from drying out. Brush the sheet with melted butter and line part of the tin with it leaving a little pastry hanging over the sides. Repeat this with another 3 or 4 sheets of pastry until the tin is completely lined. Don't worry if some bits tear, just fill the gap with another bit of buttered pastry or press the bits together.

Spoon the filling into the tin and spread out evenly. Fold the overhanging pastry into the middle and brush with butter. Butter another 3 sheets of pastry and arrange over the top to enclose the pie. Leave these layers slightly scrunched up over the top and tuck the edges of the pastry in down the sides of the tin.

Brush the top with melted butter (reserve any that is left over) and cook on a baking sheet for 45–50 minutes or until golden brown and puffed up. Pour any butter that has seeped out onto the baking sheet over the top and brush with reserved butter if there was any. Either turn out or leave in the tin or dish.

roast butternut squash with blue cheese, parma ham and walnuts

To make this into something more substantial, serve with some crusty bread and a green salad. Nice and easy to double up for a crowd too.

GET AHEAD
Prepare to the end of paragraph 2 several hours in advance and cover until required.

Serves 4

1 large butternut squash
1 bulb of garlic, cloves separated and
    unpeeled
olive oil
a little fresh sage, roughly chopped
salt and freshly ground black pepper

50 g (2 oz) creamy blue cheese such as
    Gorgonzola or dolcelatte
small handful of walnuts
few tablespoons of cream (optional)
4 slices of Parma ham
extra sage leaves to fry (optional)

HINTS AND TIPS
To fry sage leaves, heat a little olive oil in a frying pan and add four or five leaves. Fry for a few seconds on each side, remove from the pan, drain on paper towel and sprinkle with salt. Don't allow them to brown. Repeat as necessary. They crisp up when cool and will keep for two days in an airtight container.

Turk's turban squash

Preheat the oven to 200°C (400°F) gas 6.

Cut the unpeeled squash into quarters, scoop out the seeds and arrange cut side up in a shallow, greased ovenproof dish into which they fit snugly. Lightly squash the unpeeled garlic cloves under the flat blade of a large chopping knife by bashing it with your palm, and scatter them around the squash.

Sprinkle with olive oil, the sage, salt and freshly ground black pepper and cook for 45–55 minutes until soft and a little bit charred around the edges. The time will depend on the size and age of the squash.

Remove from the oven, pour a little cream over the squash if using, and crumble the cheese into the cavities and over the rest of the squash. Roughly break up or chop the walnuts and scatter over. Return to the oven for a few minutes until the cream and cheese are bubbling.

Tear the Parma ham into rough strips and drape over the squash, followed by another glug of olive oil and the fried sage leaves if using (see opposite).

vegetables & salads

Although the recipes in this chapter are accompaniments, most make perfectly good stand-alone dishes. I haven't included vegetables that just need steaming or boiling – just remember to cook anything that grows above the ground in boiling, salted water. Anything below ground goes into cold, salted water which ensures the heat has penetrated to the centre when they come up to the boil and therefore will cook evenly throughout.

crispy straw potato galettes

These are too tasty for their own good – it's almost impossible not to pick at the crispy golden bits round the edges. They make an excellent accompaniment to roast meats and game and also make a delectable starter.

Serves 4–6

900 g (2 lb) potatoes
85 g (3 oz) butter
½ tsp salt

Chives

Preheat the oven to 200°C (400°F) gas 6.

Using the grater disc of a food processor or mandolin, grate the potatoes into thin straw-like sticks. Tip into a sieve and rinse well under cold water until the water runs clear. Drain and squeeze out any excess liquid in batches, using your hands. Spread out onto a tea towel or between two layers of paper towel to dry further.

Melt the butter in a saucepan large enough to hold the potatoes. Brush a large baking sheet with some of the butter, then add the potatoes and salt to the pan. Stir until the potatoes are evenly coated with butter.

Take a tablespoonful of the mixture and mould into a rough, flattish round galette using the palms of your hands. A higgledy-piggledy edge is what you are after. Put onto the baking sheet and flatten a little. Repeat with the rest of the mixture.

Cook for 15–20 minutes or until the undersides are a rich golden brown colour, then, using a palette knife, flip each galette over and cook for a further 5–10 minutes or until crisp and golden. Keep a close eye on them as the edges can burn quite easily – particularly any wispy edge bits – and exact cooking times will depend on the thickness of your galettes.

GET AHEAD
Make in advance up to a day ahead. If preparing on the day, leave on the baking sheet ready for reheating. Reheat in a moderate oven for 5 minutes or until sizzling again, just before required.

HINTS AND TIPS
These also make a delicious starter and, if made much smaller, excellent canapés. Top with almost anything – smoked salmon, crème fraîche, spring onions or chives and caviar; beetroot (beets) and crème fraîche for vegetarians smoked mackerel or eel with horseradish…the list is endless. Warm them up before adding the topping.

Do bear in mind the galettes can burn quite easily – particularly the sticky out straw-like bits round the edges, so watch carefully.

parmentier potatoes

Half way between roast and sauté potatoes, these crunchy little cubes are irresistible. I think I cook these more than any other potatoes when entertaining, especially with roasts and game. They look wonderful piled down one side of a platter with the sliced meat overlapping down the other, or piled up high in the centre of a round platter with whole game birds or lamb cutlets arranged around the edge.

Serves 4

4 large baking sized potatoes
olive oil
few sprigs of thyme or oregano
  fresh or dried

2 cloves of garlic, crushed
salt and freshly ground black pepper

Preheat the oven to 220°C (425°F) gas 7.

Chop the rounded edges off the potatoes, leaving a straightish-sided oblong of potato. Cut this into slices roughly 2 cm (¾ in) thick horizontally, then the same thickness vertically, and then chop down into 2 cm (¾ in) dice.

Bring up to the boil in cold salted, water and simmer for 2 minutes. Drain and put into a roasting tin with a good glug of olive oil, the herbs, garlic and salt and pepper and toss well together.

Cook until golden brown and crispy, turning every so often.

GET AHEAD
Prepare, parboil and put the potatoes in the roasting tin several hours in advance, cool and cover until required.

HINTS AND TIPS
If the potatoes are ready before you need them, remove from the oven, leave them in the tin and when required reheat for a few minutes, until sizzling again.

slow-fried lemon and oregano potatoes

This recipe came about as I wanted to create potatoes to serve with fish – hence the lemon. In fact it goes with just about everything and has become a firm favourite. Lemony, sticky, golden and a little bit crispy – yum.

Serves 4–6

1 kg (2¼ lb) waxy salad potatoes
  such as 'Charlotte'
olive oil
knob of butter
2 cloves of garlic, chopped
few sprigs of fresh oregano or a
  pinch of dried

1 lemon, zest and juice
1 tsp salt
freshly ground black pepper
a few handfuls of baby spinach leaves
  (optional)

GET AHEAD
Cook the potatoes several hours in advance, leave in the pan and reheat with the spinach, if using, when required.

Slice the potatoes lengthways, roughly 3 mm (⅛ in) thick. Heat a little olive oil in a sauté pan that has a lid and add a generous knob of butter. Add the potatoes, garlic, oregano, lemon zest and juice and some salt and pepper. Toss gently to coat everything, cover with a lid and cook as slowly as possible for about an hour, turning carefully from time to time. The potatoes should be soft, golden and almost jammy and sticky. They may even fall apart slightly. If you prefer them a little more golden and crispy, cook over a high heat for a few minutes with the lid off.

Check the seasoning and if using baby spinach add it to the pan, a handful at a time, just before serving, allowing it to wilt between each addition.

spiced roast root vegetables

Slightly spicy with the addition of a little garam masala, this is one of my favourite ways of eating root vegetables. It is a very good accompaniment to stews and casseroles, adding a welcome bit of crunch and structure. Also good with game and roast meats and it is excellent for vegetarians with some sweet apricot or mango chutney and soured cream or some thick Greek yoghurt dolloped on the top.

Serves 6–8

2 parsnips
2 carrots
½ small turnip
2 onions
½ celeriac (celery) root

1 small sweet potato
1 tsp garam masala
salt and freshly ground black pepper
olive oil

GET AHEAD
Cook up to a day ahead and reheat in a hot oven.

HINTS AND TIPS
Any other root vegetables can be used and either more or less of the ones suggested.

Preheat the oven to 220°C (425°F) gas 7. Peel and chop all the vegetables into fairly even, small dice, about 2 cm (¾ in) square. Put into a large shallow roasting tin.

Sprinkle over the garam masala, salt, pepper and a good glug of olive oil. Mix with your hands to ensure that everything is well coated and spread out. Ideally the vegetables should only be one layer deep in the roasting tin, although a little bit of piling up won't matter too much as they will shrink as they cook.

Cook at the top of the preheated oven for 45–55 minutes, turning occasionally until the vegetables are soft and tender and starting to turn golden around the edges.

creamed spinach

This is one of our most favourite things and for that reason, one of the increasingly few times that I make a white sauce. Well worth the effort though – such as it is!

Serves 4

450 g (1lb) spinach, washed
salt and freshly ground black pepper
30 g (1 oz) butter

30 g (1 oz) flour
grating of nutmeg
290 ml (½ pint) milk

Put the wet spinach into a large saucepan with a little salt. No need to add water; the residual water on the leaves is plenty. Cook for a minute or two until just wilted. You may need to do this in two batches. Drain, refresh under cold water and squeeze out all the excess liquid, using your hands.

Melt the butter in a saucepan, stir in the flour to make a roux and cook for a minute. Gradually add the milk and season with salt, pepper and nutmeg. Bring up to the boil, stirring or whisking all the time until thickened. Bubble for a few minutes. Add the spinach and stir well to amalgamate. If the mixture is too thick, let it down with a little more milk and bubble up again.

GET AHEAD
Make up to 2 days in advance, cool, cover and keep in the fridge or freeze. Reheat in a saucepan with a little extra milk or in a microwave.

HINTS AND TIPS
Creamed spinach goes beautifully with lamb, steak, chicken, game and fish.

creamy baked beetroot (beets)

Delicious with chicken, beef, fish and sausages, lovely sweet beetroot (beet) is baked in a creamy sauce spiked with a little horseradish. Avoid the ready-cooked beetroot if you can and in particular the ones doused in vinegar, as they are generally overcooked and soggy with little flavour.

Beetroot

Serves 6

6 medium-sized beetroot (beets), raw
olive oil
salt and freshly ground black pepper
fresh thyme sprigs (optional)
200 ml (7 fl oz) crème fraîche

3 good tsp creamed horseradish
a few chives or chopped parsley for decorating

GET AHEAD
Roast and peel the beetroot and make the sauce up to 2 days in advance, cool, cover and chill individually. Slice and arrange the beetroot up to a day in advance but don't spoon the sauce over until just before cooking.

Preheat the oven to 200°C (400°F) gas 6. Wash the beetroot and cut off all but 5 cm (2 in) of the stems. This is important, otherwise the beetroot will 'bleed'. Tear off a large piece of foil, place the beetroot in the middle, scatter over a large glug of olive oil, some salt, black pepper and a few sprigs of thyme if using. Bring up the sides of the foil, crimping the edges together, making a loose, domed parcel. Put into a roasting tin and cook for 1½–2 hours depending on the size of the beetroot, less time if smaller. When the skins slip off easily, they are cooked.

When cool enough to handle, slip the skins off the beetroot – rubber gloves will prevent stained hands! Mix the crème fraîche and horseradish together and season with salt and freshly ground black pepper.

Slice the beetroot and arrange in concentric circles in a shallow, ovenproof dish just large enough to take the beetroot in one layer. The slices should be slightly overlapping. Spoon this mixture over the beetroot and cook for 20–25 minutes until hot and bubbling around the edges. Just before serving, scatter with snipped chives or chopped parsley if you like.

summer vegetable medley

A lovely fresh medley of lightly braised green vegetables which is a variation of the classic Petit Pois à la Française. Use this recipe as a guide, adding whichever vegetables you have to hand and don't worry too much about the quantities. Thanks to all the delicious juices, this is an ideal accompaniment to fried or grilled meats and fish. A very good vegetarian main course too.

Serves 4

*2 little gem lettuces, trimmed and halved
    through the root*
*225 g (8 oz) small broad (fava) beans,
    fresh or frozen*
*225 g (8 oz) petit pois (peas), fresh
    or frozen*
*1 bunch of spring onions, trimmed and
    cut into 2.5 cm (1 in) chunks*

*200 g (7 oz) asparagus, woody ends
    snapped off, cut into 5 cm (2 in) chunks
    and any fat spears halved*
3 sprigs of mint leaves, chopped
pinch of sugar
salt and freshly ground black pepper
splash of water
large knob of butter
double (heavy) cream (optional)

GET AHEAD
Cook several hours in advance and leave in the pan but remove the lid until cold. Reheat gently until just bubbling.

HINTS AND TIPS
As the vegetables are braised, they will not be a vivid green colour. This is how they are meant to be.

Put the lettuces cut side up in the bottom of a sauté pan or shallow casserole that has a lid. In the order that they are listed, scatter the rest of the vegetables over the top followed by the mint and sugar. Season, add a splash of water and dot with butter.

Cover, bring to the boil and simmer very gently for 10–15 minutes giving the pan the odd shake, until the vegetables are just tender. If using, stir in a little cream, bubble up, check the seasoning and serve.

Little gem lettuce

courgette (zucchini), tomato and mint sauté

A lovely melange making use of gluts of courgettes (zucchini) and tomatoes that fruit so prolifically at the same time of year. The mint ties it all together nicely. I often use this as a pasta sauce, sometimes adding basil instead of mint and it is also very good with a fillet of fried fish on top and a few crushed new potatoes.

Courgettes

Serves 4

2 large or 4 smaller courgettes (zucchini), about 400 g (14 oz)
1 large beef tomato or 2 smaller ones – 225–250 g (8–9 oz), skinned
2 sprigs of mint, leaves only
olive oil

good knob of butter
salt and freshly ground black pepper
75ml (2½ fl oz) vegetable or chicken stock

Chop the courgettes by cutting each one into quarters lengthways then into chunks no bigger than 1 cm (½ in) thick. Quarter the skinned tomato, remove and discard the seeds, cut into strips and dice the flesh. Stack up and roll the mint leaves into a cigarette shape and snip into ribbons.

Heat 1 tablespoon of olive oil and the butter in a large frying pan and add the courgettes. Season and cook over a hot flame for a minute or so until they begin to brown around the edges.

Add the mint and stock, bring up to the boil and simmer until most, but not all of the liquid has evaporated. At the last minute add the tomato, check the seasoning and lastly, swirl in a good glug of olive oil shaking the pan to emulsify the mixture. Don't add the tomato until the last minute or stir the mixture around too much once it's added as it will disintegrate to a mush.

GET AHEAD
Chop the courgettes and tomatoes any time on the day of eating. Continue just before serving.

HINTS AND TIPS
To skin a tomato, cut a small cross just though the skin, put into a bowl and pour over boiling water to cover. Leave for about 15 seconds or until the snicked skin peels back a little. The length of time will depend on the ripeness of the tomato. Remove with a slotted spoon and plunge into cold water to stop it cooking. Peel off the skin.

nasi goreng

This Southeast Asian street food can be bought on every street corner, typically for breakfast. Translated it means fried rice and is often eaten with a fried egg on top.
A very good way of using up leftovers, you can add pretty much anything that you have to hand.

Serves 4–6

3 cloves of garlic, roughly chopped
½ tsp sugar
2 small shallots, roughly chopped
2 red chillies (chili peppers), seeded
   and roughly chopped (or ½ tsp ready
   prepared)
1 tsp shrimp paste (belacan or blachan)
1 tsp coriander seeds
3 tbsp vegetable oil
200 g (7 oz) rump steak or duck breast,
   finely sliced (optional)

400 g (14 oz) raw or cooked prawns
   (shrimp) (or a mixture of both)
500 g (1 lb 2 oz) cooked rice
   (i.e., 200g / 7 oz uncooked)
2 tsp ketjap manis (sweet soy sauce)
1 tbsp tomato ketchup
1 tbsp soy sauce
1 bunch of spring onions, trimmed and
   finely chopped
fresh coriander or parsley (optional)

GET AHEAD
Make up to a day ahead, cool, cover and refrigerate. Bring back to room temperature or reheat in a wok with a little extra oil when required.

HINTS AND TIPS
Shrimp paste is available in good supermarkets and ethnic shops. Don't be put off by its smell when raw. It is transformed once cooked.

Using a pestle and mortar, small grinder or processor, combine the garlic, sugar, shallots, chillies, shrimp paste, and coriander seeds until a paste is formed.

Heat 1 tbsp of oil in a large saucepan, wok or deep frying pan and add the paste. Cook for a minute or so until fragrant. Add the steak or duck and the prawns, if raw, if using. Stir-fry for 2–3 minutes until the meat is cooked and the prawns have changed colour.

Add the remaining oil, the cold rice and cooked prawns, if using. Stir-fry, breaking up any lumps until the rice is heated through. Add the ketjap manis, tomato ketchup, soy sauce and half the spring onions and stir-fry for another minute. Tip onto a serving dish and decorate with coriander or parsley and the remaining spring onions. Serve straightaway, warm or cold.

Shallots

panzanella

Quite delectable! This classic Italian peasant tomato and bread salad is embellished here with other ingredients, adding crunch and a bit of heat. You can improvise with whatever you have to hand but the tomatoes should always be very, very ripe.

Serves 4

½ country-style loaf of bread
olive oil
salt and freshly ground black pepper
1 clove of garlic, crushed
1 large red chilli (chili pepper), halved,
* seeded and finely chopped*
3 tbsp red wine vinegar
pinch of caster (superfine granulated)
* sugar*
125 ml (4 fl oz) olive oil
450 g (1 lb) very ripe baby plum or

* cherry tomatoes, halved*
1 small red (bell) pepper, halved,
* seeded and cut into small chunks*
½ cucumber, halved and quartered
* lengthways and cut into chunks*
2 sticks of celery, finely sliced
1½ tbsp capers
4 spring onions, trimmed and chopped
½ red onion, finely sliced
2 sprigs of basil

GET AHEAD
Prepare the bread and dressing several days in advance and store in an airtight container.
  Prepare the rest of the components any time on the day but don't assemble until just before eating.

Preheat the oven to 200°C (400°F) gas 6. Tear the bread into random-sized chunks – some large, some small – and spread them onto a baking sheet or shallow roasting tin. Toss with a little olive oil and sea salt and cook until golden brown and crunchy, 5–10 minutes depending on the density of the bread. Cool. Whisk the garlic, chilli, vinegar and sugar together in a bowl with the olive oil and some seasoning.

  Pile all the remaining ingredients except the basil into a bowl, pour over the dressing, season with salt and pepper and toss together.

  To serve, arrange some of the croutons in the bottom of a large bowl or deep platter, pile on the salad and its juices and top with the remaining croutons and some torn basil leaves.

cruditées

The idea for this recipe comes from France where they do wonderful platters of seasonal vegetables accompanied by bread and perhaps a bowl of aïoli. Not really a recipe, just a platter of fresh, seasonal deliciousness. A selection of any of the following artistically arranged on a large platter makes a delicious centre-piece, either as a starter or a main course for lunch. The quantities given will serve 4–6 people for lunch and 6–8 people as a starter.

225 g (8 oz) cherry tomatoes
Halve the tomatoes and mix with a little chopped shallot, crushed garlic, a pinch of sugar, salt, pepper, basil and olive oil.

½ a small celeriac (celery root)
Peel and grate the celeriac and mix with mayonnaise and a dollop of seedy mustard.

2 large carrots
Peel and grate the carrots, mix with salt, a splash of olive oil and a few poppy seeds.

4 eggs
Coat 4 hardboiled eggs with some mayonnaise. Dust the top with a little paprika, cayenne, chopped chives or anchovy.

4 small beetroot (beets)
Bake the beetroot, wrapped in foil, with some salt and olive oil in a medium oven for 1½ hours. Peel, dice and mix with black pepper and a splash of olive oil.

1 small cucumber
Peel and cut the cucumber in half lengthways, scoop out the seeds and slice into 'boats'. Marinate with 4 tbsp white wine vinegar, 4 heaped teaspoons of sugar and a little salt for at least an hour or up to the day before.

4 baby courgettes (zucchini)
Slice lengthways either with a peeler or mandolin and dress with a little olive oil, lemon juice and seasoning.

1 bulb of fennel
Remove the tough outer layer, finely slice using a mandolin and dress with a little olive oil, lemon juice and seasoning.

HINTS AND TIPS
Salami, Parma ham, radishes (with their green tops left on), artichokes (fresh or from a jar, chargrilled in oil) are other suggestions. A bowl of aïoli (garlicky mayonnaise) would also be good, as would some basil tops or pea shoots to decorate.

fresh pea, parma ham and feta salad

Tender, sweet, freshly podded, minty peas combined with chunks of salty feta cheese and sweet dressing. Delicious eaten as a salad or with lamb – rump or chops would be good, barbecued or roasted.

Serves 4–6

450 g (1 lb) fresh unshelled peas
(or use frozen)
4 slices of Parma ham, halved
lengthways and cut into thin batons
1 bunch of spring onions, trimmed and
sliced into rings
10 mint leaves, chopped
110 g (4 oz) feta cheese

Dressing
1 tsp Dijon mustard
1 tsp palm or brown sugar
1 tbsp sherry vinegar
3 tbsp olive oil
salt and freshly ground black pepper

GET AHEAD
Cook the peas, slice the Parma ham and the spring onions up to a day ahead, cover and chill individually. Assemble the salad an hour or so in advance but don't dress until the last minute.

Potatoes, mint, peas and spinach

Shell the peas and cook until just tender in boiling salted water. Drain and cool under cold water. Dry on paper towel and put into a mixing bowl.

Add the Parma ham, spring onions, mint and two tablespoons of the dressing. Mix well together. Check the seasoning and add more dressing if you think it needs it although you won't need it all. Spoon into a serving dish, scatter the feta cheese, broken into chunks, over the top and serve.

oriental salad

Fresh, crisp and flavourful, this is a lovely accompaniment to oriental-style food. It is also very good with cold meats of any kind and I think looks at its best when piled up onto a plate or platter. Use your own judgement quantity-wise depending on which ingredients you have.

Use a selection of any or all of the following:

pak choi, shredded into thick ribbons
Chinese leaves, shredded into thick
  ribbons
bean sprouts
mangetout (snow peas), raw and thinly
  sliced on the diagonal
watercress
noodles, egg or rice
spring onions, trimmed and cut into
  thin strips lengthways
red chilli (chili pepper), halved, seeded
  and sliced

a good handful of coriander, leaves and
  fine stems roughly chopped
salted cashews or peanuts, plain or dry
  roast, roughly chopped if you like
toasted sesame seeds

Dressing
1 tbsp palm or brown sugar
1 tbsp toasted sesame oil
juice of 1 lime
1 tbsp soy sauce
½ tbsp fish sauce (nam pla)

GET AHEAD
Prepare the salad several hours in advance, cover and keep in the fridge undressed. Make the dressing up to a day in advance.

Mix your chosen salad ingredients together in a large bowl, leaving out the peanuts and sesame seeds. Just before serving toss with a little of the dressing – you may not need it all so add it in stages. Lastly, scatter the nuts and seeds over, if using.

swiss chard with chickpeas and chilli (chili pepper)

I grow a variety of Swiss Chard called Bright Lights which produces the most amazing jewel-coloured stems from brilliant yellow and green to shocking pink and bright orange. The more typical green and white chard is just as good and if that proves elusive, use spinach instead but you will need to up the quantity. Serve hot as a vegetable or cold as a salad.

Swiss chard

Serves 4

450 g (1 lb) Swiss chard
olive oil
2 cloves of garlic, chopped
1 red chilli (chili pepper), chopped

salt and freshly ground black pepper
1 x 400 g (14 oz) tin (can) of chickpeas,
*   drained and rinsed*

GET AHEAD
Prepare to the end of paragraph 1 anytime on the day of eating. Cook just before required.

HINTS AND TIPS
A large pinch of ground cumin added with the chilli and garlic adds a nice extra spicy flavour. Good with a fillet of fried fish on top such as sea bass, cod or haddock.

Chop the stems off the chard and cut into 2.5 cm (1 in) chunks. Wash well and drain. Stack the leaves into piles with the larger leaves at the bottom, roll into tight cigarette shapes and slice into fine ribbons. Wash and drain; keep separate from the stems.

Heat the olive oil in a large sauté pan or wok, add the stalks and stir-fry for about five minutes or until beginning to soften. Season with salt and pepper. Add the leaves a handful at a time and stir until just wilted. Tip into a sieve and leave to drain.

Meanwhile, heat a splash more oil in the pan (no need to wash it) and add the garlic and chilli. Stir-fry for a minute then stir in the chick peas. Return the chard to the pan, mix everything together well, check the seasoning and serve with a swirl of olive oil over the top.

parmesan-baked fennel

This is such a good accompaniment to most meats and fish and very good in its own right, perhaps with the Roasted Red (Bell) Pepper Sauce (page 179) or a tomato sauce. Swap the butter for olive oil if you prefer or use a mixture of both.

Serves 4–6

4 large heads of fennel
salt and freshly ground black pepper
splash of lemon juice
good knob of butter

4 tbsp freshly grated Parmesan cheese
(see page 176)
few dried breadcrumbs (see page 176)

GET AHEAD
Prepare to the end of paragraph 2 up to a day ahead. Cool, cover and chill. Do make sure you cool the fennel completely before topping with the rest of the ingredients and bring back to room temperature before cooking.

Preheat the oven to 220°C (425°F) gas 7. Butter a shallow ovenproof dish, just big enough to accommodate the fennel. It's fine if it's in two layers in some places but bear in mind that it all needs to come into contact with some of the Parmesan.

Trim the fennel, discarding the stems and tough outside layer and scrape away any stringy bits with a potato peeler. Reserve the green fronds and chop them roughly. Cut the bulbs in half through the root and then each half into about three wedges, depending on their size. Cook in boiling salted water with a splash of lemon juice until just tender when stabbed with a knife, about 5–10 minutes. Drain well and blot dry on paper towel. Arrange in the gratin dish and sprinkle with half the chopped fennel fronds and the Parmesan, dot with some butter and finally scatter over a few dried breadcrumbs.

Bake for 15–20 minutes or until the cheese is melted and pale golden.

desserts

Easy, make-ahead and delicious! There is nothing like finishing off a meal with something sweet, whether it's rich chocolate, tangy fruit or creamy indulgence.

pineapple and lime carpaccio

One of the most simple and refreshing desserts imaginable. Ice-cold wafer-thin slices of juicy pineapple with a citrus kick from the lime. I like to serve this with Stem Ginger Ice Cream (see page 146).

Serves 8

1 large ripe pineapple
zest and juice of 1 lime

Using a large, sharp chopping knife cut the top and bottom off the pineapple. Discard the bottom but reserve the top.

Stand the pineapple on a chopping board and working from top to bottom, carefully slice the thick skin off in sections following the contours of the fruit. Slice the pineapple flesh into the thinnest possible slices. Arrange in slightly overlapping concentric circles on a large flat serving platter.

Scatter over the lime zest and juice and sit the leafy top of the pineapple in the centre (optional). Cover, chill and serve straight from the fridge.

GET AHEAD
Prepare up to the end of paragraph 2 up to a day in advance, cover and refrigerate.
Add zest and juice several hours in advance.

HINTS AND TIPS
If the pineapple is not ripe and therefore not sweet enough, dredge some icing (powdered) sugar over the top at the same time as the lime. A guide to whether a pineapple is ripe is to smell the bottom. The sweeter it smells, the riper the pineapple.

stem ginger ice cream

A nice and easy old-fashioned-style ice cream that is richer and creamier than the custard-based ones (which contain eggs and need cooking). Ice crystals are less likely to form and this is what makes it so delectably smooth.

Serves 6–8

568 ml (1 pint) double (heavy) cream
125 ml (4 fl oz) sweetened condensed milk
3 tbsp stem ginger syrup
½ tsp vanilla extract

pinch of salt
4 pieces of stem ginger, finely chopped

Whisk the cream, condensed milk, syrup, vanilla extract and salt until it just holds its shape in soft peaks. Stir in the stem ginger. Either pour the mixture into a chilled ice-cream machine and churn according to the appliance instructions, or still freeze by pouring into a shallow container, covering and freezing for 1½–2 hours or until it has frozen around the edge of the container. Whisk the ice cream with an electric beater, whisk or fork until the ice crystals are broken up. Cover, return to the freezer and repeat twice more.

Scrape the ice cream into a shallow plastic freezer box into which it fits snugly. Cover with greaseproof paper or clingfilm placed directly onto the ice cream to exclude any air. (This stops ice crystals forming.) Cover with a lid and freeze until firm. Overnight is best.

GET AHEAD
The ice cream will keep happily in the freezer for several weeks. Remember to cover it directly onto the surface, as well as with a lid.

HINTS AND TIPS
If you are short of time just pour the ice cream into a container and freeze without beating. Although still delicious, the finished product won't be quite as creamy. Scoop into balls and arrange in a bowl any time after the ice cream has spent a night in the freezer and refreeze until required. Or freeze in a loaf tin lined with clingfilm (wet the tin first) and cut into slices.

lemon posset

Three ingredients, three minutes cooking time and a sublime, luscious velvety result. A posset is one of the oldest known English puddings dating back to medieval times and is even mentioned in Shakespeare's *Macbeth*. Some shortbread (see page 156) would be a lovely accompaniment.

Autumn raspberries

Serves 8

600 ml (1 pint) double (heavy) cream
155 g (5½ oz) caster (superfine
  granulated) sugar

juice of 2 lemons
fresh raspberries and/or blueberries to
  decorate

GET AHEAD
Make up to 2 days in advance

HINTS AND TIPS
Don't cook the cream in a non-stick pan as this causes it to form a scorched skin on the bottom. Stirring occasionally to help dissolve the sugar as the cream is heating will help to prevent scalding too.

Bring the cream and sugar up to the boil, stirring occasionally, in a pan large enough to allow plenty of space for the cream to expand whilst boiling.

Boil rapidly for exactly 3 minutes. Remove from the heat, whisk in the lemon juice and pour into glasses or small pots. Allow to cool, then cover and refrigerate for at least six hours until set, but better still overnight.

Decorate with raspberries or blueberries and a dusting of icing (powdered) sugar.

spiced orange panna cotta with blueberry compote

Minimum effort for maximum impact! Panna Cotta (cooked cream in Italian) is so easy to make especially when using leaf gelatine. This recipe produces a light, barely set amalgamation which is still easy to turn out.

Serves 8

400 ml (14 fl oz) full fat milk
400 ml (14 fl oz) double (heavy) cream
4 tbsp caster (superfine granulated) sugar
1 cinnamon stick, plus 1 to decorate (optional)
2 oranges, grated zest only
2 tbsp Cointreau (or other orange liqueur)

4 leaves of gelatine (for powdered gelatine, see Hints and Tips)

For the compote
2 tbsp granulated sugar
3 tbsp orange juice
300 g (11oz) blueberries

Put the milk, cream and sugar into a saucepan with the cinnamon stick split into shards lengthways, the orange zest and Cointreau. Slowly bring to the boil and simmer for five minutes. Remove from the heat and strain into a measuring jug squeezing the juices from the solids with the back of a spoon. Allow to cool slightly.

Put the gelatine leaves into a bowl of cold water and leave for five minutes to soften. Remove from the water, squeeze out any excess liquid and whisk into the cream mixture. Pour into 8 mini pudding moulds, ramekins or small dishes. Cool, cover and refrigerate until set.

For the compote, heat the sugar with the orange juice until dissolved. Boil fast for 30 seconds then add the blueberries and stir gently over the heat, without breaking them up, just until they are all coated and their juice begins to run into the syrup. Cool, cover and refrigerate.

To serve in their dishes, spoon some poached berries over the top, or, to turn out, dip the moulds into hot water, loosen around the edges with your finger to create a vacuum and un-mould onto individual plates. Spoon a little of the blueberry compote onto each plate and decorate with a shard of cinnamon stick if using.

GET AHEAD
Make both the panna cotta and the compote up to 3–4 days in advance.

HINTS AND TIPS
Instead of a compote, purée and sieve some fresh or frozen berries with a little icing (powdered) sugar to make a sauce. Or serve with some orange segments.

To use powdered gelatine instead of leaf gelatine, sprinkle 3 level tsp gelatine over 4 tbsp water in a small saucepan. Leave for a few minutes to sponge/bloom. The mixture will become solid and look like a sponge. Slowly dissolve the gelatine over a very gentle heat. Do not boil. Whisk the gelatine into the cream mixture well. Continue according to the directions. If you can, do use leaf gelatine. It is foolproof and much easier than powdered!

plum frangipane tarts

Every year we have a glut of plums and these tarts have become favourites at plum time. The glaze on the top gives them that lovely French patisserie look and any frangipane spillages over the edge just add to their rustic charm. The plums don't have to be ripe.

Victoria plums

Makes 8

*1 x 375 g (13 oz) ready-rolled puff
pastry sheet, all butter if possible
8 plums, halved and stoned (pitted)
(or 6 if large)
caster (superfine granulated) sugar
for dredging
5 tbsp apricot jam or apricot baking
glaze (see hints and tips)
icing (powdered) sugar*

For the frangipane

*50 g (2 oz) butter, softened
50 g (2 oz) caster (superfine granulated)
sugar
1 small egg, beaten
50 g (2 oz) ground almonds
15 g (½ oz) plain (all-purpose) flour*

GET AHEAD
The tarts can be made entirely in advance and eaten cold or warmed for a few minutes. Alternatively make to the end of paragraph 2 several hours in advance and cooked when required.

HINTS AND TIPS
Apricot baking glaze is now readily available – the next best option is jam with no bits if you can find it. Alternatively, buy cheaper brands of apricot jam, as they tend to have fewer bits. However, this means they might be runnier when melted, so go easy on the water until you see the melted consistency.

Preheat the oven to 220°C (425°F) gas 7. Unroll the pastry and cut into 8 even-sized rectangles. Place on a baking sheet lined with silicone paper and using the point of a knife carefully score a rim about 1 cm (½ in) around each rectangle. Chill.

Make the frangipane by mixing all the ingredients together in a processor or by hand. Divide the mixture between the eight rectangles and spread evenly leaving the rims clear. Cut the plums into wedges and arrange artistically, according to their size, cut side down and gently pushed into the frangipane on each tart.

Dust well all over with caster sugar, including the pastry rim and cook for 10–15 minutes or until the pastry and frangipane are puffed up and golden brown. You may need to turn the baking sheet round at half time for even cooking.

Melt the jam with 1 tablespoon of water and brush all over the tarts when they come out of the oven to form a shiny glaze. Make sure there are no gaps. Just before serving, dust with icing sugar and eat warm or cold with vanilla ice cream, crème fraîche or double (heavy) cream.

sticky rhubarb and ginger cake

A pudding or a cake, warm, or cold – it's up to you. As the flavours of rhubarb and elderflower are a marriage made in heaven, I like to serve this with elderflower-infused crème fraîche.

Serves 8

110 g (4 oz) butter, softened
110 g (4 oz) self-raising (self-rising) flour
110 g (4 oz) caster (superfine granulated) sugar
½ tsp baking powder
2 large eggs
4–5 sticks of young rhubarb, cut into 2.5cm (1 in) chunks

2 large bulbs of stem ginger, thinly sliced, plus a little of their syrup
2–3 tbsp demerara (light brown) sugar, plus a little extra
icing (powdered) sugar

GET AHEAD
Make up to 2 days in advance, cool, cover and store in the fridge or freeze.

HINTS AND TIPS
Eat at room temperature or warmed gently in a medium oven for 15 minutes or so before required.

Preheat the oven to 160°C (325°F) gas 3. Grease and line the base of a 20 cm (8 in) cake tin with a disc of greaseproof paper.

Place all the ingredients except the rhubarb, ginger, demerara and icing sugar into the bowl of a food processor and blitz for 20–25 seconds until well mixed. Spoon the mixture into the prepared tin and spread evenly. Arrange the rhubarb pieces on top, pushing them slightly into the raw cake mixture. Dot the slices of stem ginger between the rhubarb and drizzle over some of the syrup – about 2 teaspoons. Scatter the top with demerara sugar to almost cover, but not entirely.

Bake for 45 minutes to 1 hour. Test by sticking a skewer into the middle. If it comes out clean, the cake is cooked. Leave in the tin for five minutes before turning out onto a wire cooling rack. Peel off the paper and scatter over some demerara sugar. Dust with icing sugar before serving.

pimm's jellies

Elegant and deceptively easy, these jellies are an inexpensive way to feed a lot of people. Make them in pretty glasses or tea cups, turn them out of moulds or make one large terrine.

Serves 8

150 ml (5 fl oz) Pimm's No 1 Cup
150 ml (5 fl oz) ginger ale
300 ml (½ pint) lemonade
5 leaves of gelatine (for powdered gelatine, see Hints and Tips)
450 g (1 lb) mixed soft fruit such as strawberries, raspberries, blueberries and cherries

To serve
1 tub of crème fraîche
runny honey
edible lavender flowers, fresh or dried (optional)

Gently warm the Pimm's, ginger ale and lemonade in a saucepan. It doesn't need to be brought up to boiling point, just warmed through. Soak the gelatine leaves in a bowl of cold water for 5 minutes.

Meanwhile, gently combine the fruit in a mixing bowl. Strawberries and cherries might need cutting into smaller pieces, as all the fruit should be roughly the same size. Divide between 8 moulds, glasses or little dishes.

Squeeze the water out of the softened gelatine and whisk into the Pimm's mixture. Pour into a jug then over the fruit. Cool, cover and refrigerate, preferably overnight.

Mix some honey, to taste, into the crème fraîche and stir in a few lavender flowers, if using.

If using moulds, hold them under a hot tap or dip into a bowl of hot water for a few seconds to loosen the jellies and turn out by inverting onto individual plates. Serve straight from the fridge with the honey and lavender cream and Lavender and Lemon Shortbread (see page 156).

GET AHEAD
Make up to 3 days ahead and turn out, if using moulds, just before serving.

HINTS AND TIPS
To make this into a terrine line a 1.2 litre (2 pint) terrine or loaf tin with an oversized piece of clingfilm. Put the fruit into the terrine and then pour over the Pimm's mixture. Cool, cover with the overlapping clingfilm and refrigerate. Either serve whole as a centrepiece, perhaps surrounded with fresh berries or in slices on individual plates.

To use powdered gelatine instead of leaf gelatine, sprinkle 4 level tsp gelatine over 4 tbsp water in a small saucepan. Leave for a few minutes to sponge/bloom. The mixture will become solid and look like a sponge. Slowly dissolve the gelatine over a very gentle heat. Do not boil. Whisk the gelatine into the Pimm's mixture. Continue according to the directions. If you can, do use leaf gelatine. It is foolproof and much easier than powdered!

chocolate and berry pavlova

Pavlovas are incredibly easy and quick to make and an excellent, impressive and inexpensive way of feeding a lot of people. I have suggested a berry compote here for the filling, but when in season, fresh berries of any kind would be lovely. Just scatter over the top and dust with icing (powdered) sugar.

Serves 8–10

4 egg whites
a pinch of salt
280 g (10 oz) caster (superfine granulated) sugar
1 tsp cornflour (cornstarch)
1 tsp unsweetened cocoa powder plus extra for dusting

1 tsp vanilla extract
1 tsp white wine vinegar
500 g (1 lb 2 oz) frozen mixed berries
50 g (2 oz) good-quality plain or white chocolate
425 ml (¾ pint) double (heavy) cream
icing (powdered) sugar for dusting

Preheat the oven to 140°C (275°F) gas 1 and line a flat baking sheet with foil.

Whisk the egg whites with a pinch of salt until stiff, then add 225 g (8 oz) of the sugar, a tablespoon at a time, whisking it in well between each addition. The mixture will be very thick and shiny. When all the sugar is incorporated add the cornflour, cocoa powder, vanilla essence and vinegar and whisk well again.

Pile the mixture onto the lined baking sheet and mould it into a flattish round shape, roughly 20–25 cm (8–10 in) across and 4 cm (1½ in) deep. Make a dip in the middle using a metal spoon. Cook for 45 minutes, then turn the oven off leaving the pavlova inside until cold, without opening the door. Carefully peel it off the foil.

Put the frozen berries into a non-reactive pan with the rest of the sugar. Warm gently over a low heat, just until the fruit has thawed, trying not to break it up. Tip into a sieve over a bowl and leave to drain for 15 minutes or so. Pour the juice back into the pan and boil fast, giving it the odd stir, until it has reduced to a syrupy consistency and just coats the back of the wooden spoon. Leave to cool. It will thicken up much more when cold.

Melt the chocolate in a small bowl suspended over a pan of hot water or in a microwave and carefully brush over the inside of the pavlova. Dust the outside with cocoa powder, then icing sugar.

Whip the cream lightly into soft peaks and spoon into the centre of the pavlova. Mix the berries and the sauce together and spoon over the top.

GET AHEAD
The pavlova can be made several weeks in advance, wrapped tightly in clingfilm and kept somewhere cool and dry. The chocolate can be brushed over a few days in advance.

Make the compote several days in advance and keep the fruit and sauce covered separately in the fridge, or freeze. Only mix together just before using.

The cream can be whipped as early as you like on the day but should be under-whipped as it will thicken up whilst in the fridge.

HINTS AND TIPS
Leave out the cocoa if you prefer and the chocolate too. Cracks don't matter at all and most of them can be concealed by the filling if you so wish.

lavender and lemon shortbread

Perfectly delicious on its own or as an accompaniment to ice cream, fruit fools or the Pimm's Jellies (see page 153). Use fresh lavender stems to decorate if you have them.

(see page 153)

GET AHEAD
This keeps happily in an airtight container for several weeks. It also freezes beautifully.

HINTS AND TIPS
Lavender-flavoured sugar can be used instead of lavender flowers. Just infuse a jar of caster sugar with a sprig or two of lavender.

Makes 16 wedges

175 g (6 oz) butter, softened
85 g (3 oz) caster (superfine granulated) sugar
1 tbsp edible lavender flowers, dried or 2 tbsp fresh

1 lemon, zest only
85 g (3 oz) cornflour (cornstarch)
175 g (6 oz) plain (all-purpose) flour
caster (superfine granulated) sugar for dusting

Lavender

Preheat the oven to 150°C (300°F) gas 2. Cream with a wooden spoon or process the butter, sugar and lavender together until light and creamy. Add the lemon zest, cornflour and flour and stir or process until the mixture begins to come together into a dough.

Press into a loose-bottomed 20 cm (8 in) cake tin and smooth out evenly using a palette knife.

Cook for 40 minutes until just firm and biscuit-coloured. Whilst still hot, cut the shortbread into 16 wedges using a round-bladed knife. Scatter with a little caster sugar and leave in the tin to cool.

creamy white chocolate pots

Puddings don't get much easier than this. Don't be tempted to smooth over the tops of the pots – just spoon in the mixture and leave it to form its own pattern.

GET AHEAD
Make to the end of paragraph 2 up to 4 days in advance.

Serves 6

200 g (7 oz) best quality white chocolate
200 g (7 oz) crème fraîche
200 g (7 oz) Greek yoghurt

a few blueberries, redcurrants,
* raspberries, strawberries, passion fruit,*
* or other soft fruit*
icing (powdered) sugar to decorate

Break the chocolate into a mixing bowl. Suspend it over a saucepan of hot water until melted. Do not let the bottom of the bowl come into contact with the water.

Stir the crème fraîche into the chocolate, followed by the yoghurt and mix together until smooth. Spoon into six small pots, ramekins or glasses. Cover and leave to set in the fridge for 4 hours or overnight if possible.

Just before serving, top with your chosen fruit and dust with icing sugar. If you have no fruit to hand, a drizzle of honey would be a good alternative.

ginger creams with pistachio brittle

An easy, gingery sort of crème brûlée topped with pistachio brittle. Try snapping the brittle into random shapes and handing it round in a small pretty dish after cheese instead of a pudding, or with coffee.

Makes 8

6 tbsp ginger preserve
6 egg yolks
450 ml (16 fl oz) double (heavy) cream
175 g (6 oz) granulated sugar

3 tbsp water
100 g (3½ oz) pistachio nuts, shelled
    and roughly crushed
icing (powdered) sugar (optional)

GET AHEAD
Make the ginger creams up to 4 days in advance. The brittle can be made weeks in advance as it keeps almost indefinitely in an airtight container.

Preheat the oven to 180°C (350°F) gas 4. Put 8 ramekins or small ovenproof dishes into a deep roasting tin. Boil a kettle of water.

Whisk the ginger preserve and egg yolks together in a mixing bowl until pale. Bring the cream to just below boiling point and pour over the egg mixture, whisking all the time. The mixture will thicken slightly. Transfer to a jug and pour into the dishes. Put the roasting tin into the oven and carefully pour in enough boiling water to come roughly half-way up the sides of the dishes.

Cook for 20–25 minutes or until just set with a slight wobble in the middle, bearing in mind that the custards will continue to cook a little in the residual heat once out of the oven. Remove from the water, cool, cover and refrigerate overnight.

Whilst the custards are cooking, make the brittle. Lightly oil a baking sheet or have ready a piece of silicone paper. Put the sugar and water into a saucepan and cook over a low heat, giving the odd very gentle stir, until the sugar has dissolved. Turn up the heat and boil fast until the sugar caramelises into a deep golden colour. Quickly add the pistachios, stir and tip out immediately onto the baking sheet or paper, spreading the mixture out as thinly as possible. Leave to cool.

Serve the creams straight from the fridge, dusted with icing sugar if you like. Bash, snap or break the brittle into random-sized pieces and scatter over the top or arrange shards sticking out at an angle.

individual summer puddings

A classic English pudding which is easy to make and a good way of using up gluts of summer berries.

Serves 4

500 g (1 lb 2 oz) fresh mixed summer berries (not strawberries), plus a few extra to decorate
4 tbsp water
5 tbsp granulated sugar

1 uncut white loaf, a few days old
crème fraîche, double (heavy) or clotted cream, to serve

GET AHEAD
Make up to 3 days in advance, or freeze.

Put the berries into a non-reactive saucepan with the water and granulated sugar. Cook over a gentle heat until the juices begin to run if they are fresh, or they have thawed all the way through if frozen. Carefully tip into a sieve suspended over a bowl.

Meanwhile, wet 4 mini pudding basins and line with a generous piece of clingfilm, making sure there is enough excess hanging over the edges for folding over the top. Slice the bread into thin slices and using a pastry cutter cut out 4 small discs for the bottom of the basins and 4 slightly larger ones for the top.

Dip one side of the small discs into the sieved syrup and put dipped side down into the bottom of the basins. Cut out some oblong-shaped pieces of bread and repeat the process using them to line the sides. There should be no gaps so you will need to cut bits of bread to size.

Fill with the berries and top each basin with the syrup-dipped larger disc, dipped side uppermost. Press the lids down onto the berries and fold the excess clingfilm over the top. Put onto a plate, cover with another plate and put a weight on top of that. Chill for at least 4 hours although overnight is best. Reserve any leftover syrup.

Peel back the clingfilm, then turn the puddings out onto individual plates or one large one. Remove the clingfilm, pour over a little of the leftover syrup and decorate with some fresh berries. Any extra syrup can be handed around separately in a jug.

individual chocolate truffle and strawberry tartlets

These look wonderful if served on a large platter interspersed with strawberries dipped in white, milk and plain (semi-sweet) chocolate and/or other soft fruits. It is a bit of a cheat as I have used ready-made tartlet cases which can be filled hours in advance without going soggy.

Ready-to-eat tartlets

Serves 8

150 g (5½ oz) plain (semi-sweet) chocolate, minimum 70% cocoa solids
225 ml (8 fl oz) double (heavy) cream
8 individual ready-made sweet tartlet cases (I buy these from M&S)
200 g (7 oz) crème fraîche
8 strawberries or a small punnet (package) of raspberries
icing (powdered) sugar
Cadbury's Flake (chocolate shavings) (optional)

To decorate (optional)
1 punnet (package) of strawberries
plain (semi-sweet), milk and white chocolate
other soft fruits such as redcurrants on the stem, blueberries, raspberries or cherries

GET AHEAD
Fill the tartlet cases with chocolate up to a day ahead. Dip the strawberries up to a day ahead, if using, cover and refrigerate.

HINTS AND TIPS
For dipping, choose very fresh strawberries with a good green hull and stem. Simply melt the different chocolates in small separate bowls and holding onto the green stalk, dip the strawberries to coat the bottom half. Put onto silicone or greaseproof paper and leave to set.

Break up the chocolate and heat gently with the double cream in a small saucepan, until the chocolate has melted. Pour into the tartlet cases. Allow to cool and set.

Spoon a dollop of crème fraîche onto the top of each tartlet, making sure that a little of the chocolate mixture is still showing around the edges. Pile either whole or sliced strawberries or raspberries onto the top. Dust with icing sugar and Cadbury's flake, if using, and serve.

quick nibbles
& drinks

The perfect canapé should be small, no bigger than one mouthful – anything that requires biting into is too big in my view, and is potentially fraught with social problems such as dripping, dribbling and dropping!

blue cheese and poppy seed biscuits

Dangerously tempting and incredibly handy to have up your sleeve, these delicious, little biscuits (see page 167) couldn't be easier to make and don't even require rolling out.

Makes about 50

110 g (4 oz) self-raising (self-rising) flour
110 g (4 oz) butter
large pinch mustard powder
50 g (2 oz) blue cheese, crumbled
50 g (2 oz) mature Cheddar
  finely grated

1 tsp poppy seeds
1 tsp salt and freshly ground black
  pepper

Preheat the oven to 200°C (400°F) gas 6. Process the flour and butter until it resembles breadcrumbs. Add the mustard powder, cheeses, poppy seeds and salt and pepper and process briefly, just enough to bind the mixture together.

On a lightly floured surface, roll the mixture into two or three fat sausages about 2.5 cm (1 in) in diameter, using your hands. Wrap tightly with clingfilm, twisting the ends to keep the sausage in shape. Chill for at least an hour before using, or freeze.

Unwrap and slice into discs about the thickness of a 2p coin (similar in size to a U.S. quarter). Place on a baking sheet lined with silicone paper, or greased, leaving room for each biscuit to expand a little. Cook for 5–7 minutes or until golden brown. Using a palette knife transfer to a wire cooling rack.

GET AHEAD
The raw dough will keep up to 4 days in the fridge or can be frozen. The cooked biscuits can be stored in an airtight container for several weeks, or frozen. I like to warm cooked biscuits that have been frozen in the oven just long enough to take the 'taint' of the freezer off them. Cool before eating.

HINTS AND TIPS
I often hand round the biscuits after the dessert, instead of cheese.

blinis with smoked salmon

Much as I would like to, I can't claim this recipe as mine. I have been making these delicious blinis for years from a recipe scribbled on a scrap of paper. Excellent as canapés, or as a starter if made larger, and so much nicer than ready-made blinis. Keep up the Russian theme by serving with shot glasses of Iced Lemon Vodka (page 173).

Makes around 48 small cocktail blinis

85 g (3 oz) plain (all-purpose) flour
30 g (1 oz) buckwheat flour
*1 level tsp bicarbonate of soda
   (baking soda)*
1 level tsp cream of tartar
pinch of salt
1 egg, beaten

225–300 ml (8–10 fl oz) milk
2 tsp butter, melted
pinch of sugar
vegetable oil
*smoked salmon, crème fraîche, Avruga
   or Onuga caviar (optional), chopped
   spring onion and chives, to serve*

GET AHEAD
Make the blinis up to 3 days ahead, interleave with greaseproof paper or clingfilm, cover and refrigerate or freeze. If freezing, warm them in the oven before using to freshen them up. They take no time at all to thaw.

Put both flours, bicarbonate of soda, cream of tartar and salt into a food processor. In a jug beat together the egg, milk, butter and sugar.

With the processor running, gradually pour some of this mixture onto the flour until it starts to form a thick, smooth, lump-free paste. Scrape around the sides of the bowl with a spatula to release any flour that is stuck and process again briefly. Add more of the milk mixture with the machine running, but don't add it all at once as it may not all be needed. The finished batter should be as thick as double (heavy) cream. Pour into a jug or bowl and let it stand for at least 30 minutes.

Heat a pancake or frying pan and grease with an oiled piece of paper towel. Thin the batter if necessary.

Drop teaspoonfuls of the batter into the pan, 3 or 4 at a time, depending on the size of the pan, leaving them space to expand a little. (They should be one mouthful size.) When bubbles appear on the top, flip over with a palette knife and cook for a few moments until the underside is golden brown. If using straight away, keep the blinis warm in a napkin or layers of paper towel. Repeat with the rest of the batter, wiping the pan with oil between each batch.

Serve the blinis with a ribbon of smoked salmon on top, followed by a dollop of crème fraîche mixed with a chopped spring onion or two and finally a teaspoon of Avruga caviar, if using and/or some chopped chives.

sticky spiced nuts

Having been given a jar of quite the most delicious spiced nuts for Christmas, I tried to recreate them. Here is my version – a little different from the original but hopefully just as good. I think a jar of these, perhaps tied with some pretty ribbon, makes a lovely present and a nice change from a jar of marmalade!

Makes approximately 2 jam jars

½ tsp salt
½ tsp ground cumin
½ tsp ground coriander
½ tsp chilli (chili pepper) powder
½ tsp harissa paste
1 tbsp granulated sugar

1 tbsp vegetable oil
1 tbsp runny honey
200 g (7 oz) almonds, or half-and-half almonds and pecans, skin-on

GET AHEAD
The nuts will last for at least 2 weeks in a jar or covered container.

In a small bowl mix together all the ingredients, except for the nuts. Get ready a baking sheet either greased or lined with silicone paper.

Put the nuts into a dry frying pan, add the spice mixture and stir over a medium heat until the mixture has melted and is beginning to caramelise to a deep golden brown and coat the nuts. Tip onto the baking sheet, spread out well, sprinkle with a little extra salt and leave to cool.

parma ham and parmesan palmiers

Something else that's almost impossible to make enough of, these tasty crisp little puff pastry canapés are a savoury version of the French sweet pastries of the same name. Also good as an accompaniment to vegetable soups.

Makes about 52 palmiers

1 packet of ready-rolled puff pastry
Dijon mustard
*2 tbsp grated Parmesan cheese, plus a
   little extra*

6 slices of Parma ham
1 egg, beaten with a pinch of salt

GET AHEAD
Prepare the rolls, before slicing, up to a day ahead or freeze. Alternatively slice the palmiers (after a period of firming up in the fridge), arrange on a baking sheet ready to cook, cover and refrigerate or freeze. Thaw before cooking which will take less than an hour.

Preheat the oven to 200°C (400°F) gas 6. Unroll the pastry with the long edge closest to you (landscape) and cut in half vertically. Spread each half with a little Dijon mustard followed by 1 tablespoon of Parmesan on each. Lay three slices of Parma ham on each half horizontally, starting at the top of the short edge. This should cover the pastry entirely.

Taking one half of pastry at a time, fold the longest edges in on each side by about 2.5 cm (1 in). Brush the two strips of bare pastry with the beaten egg wash and fold each side over again in the same way. The two folded edges should have met in the middle and be touching. Brush well with egg glaze and fold one side inwards over the other to form a long flattish roll. Wrap in clingfilm and refrigerate for at least half an hour. Repeat with the other half of pastry.

Trim the ends off each roll and using a very sharp knife, carefully cut each one into roughly ½ cm (¼ in) slices. Lay on a baking sheet, greased, or lined with silicone paper, leaving enough space for each one to expand a little. Scatter over a little extra grated Parmesan. Cook for 6–10 minutes or until golden brown and crispy. Scatter over a little more Parmesan if you like and serve whilst still warm.

elderflower cordial

This is so much nicer than the bought variety and very easy and cheap to make. The citric acid stops the cordial from fermenting and can be bought from chemists (pharmacists). Make sure the pretty, lacy flowers are creamy white and fresh. Pink elderflowers, found on black elder (*Sambucus nigra*), produce the prettiest pink cordial.

3 lemons
50 g (2 oz) citric acid powder
1.3 kg (3 lb) granulated sugar

1.7 l (3 pints) boiling water
25 fresh elderflower heads

GET AHEAD
The cordial will last for several months in the fridge if unopened. It also freezes very well. Freeze with the lids off the bottles and leave a 5 cm (2 in) gap at the top to allow for expansion during freezing, then screw on the lids or cork the bottles.

Put the lemon zest and juice, citric acid, sugar and boiling water into a large bowl. Stir until dissolved.

Add the elderflower heads, stir well, cover and leave for 3 days, giving it the odd stir when you're passing.

Sieve and then strain through muslin or paper towel. Pour into sterilized bottles. Because of the high sugar content this will keep in the fridge for a long time.

Elderflowers

Stirring the mixture

iced lemon vodka

Delicious served straight from the freezer in shot glasses and especially good as an accompaniment to Russian starters such as Jellied Borscht (see page 14). Try to buy vodka in an attractive bottle. Failing that, decant it into an elegant bottle, which also turns it into a lovely present.

1 unwaxed lemon
1 bottle of vodka

Pare the zest from the lemon using a small knife or potato peeler, making sure there is no white pith on the zest, as this is bitter. Add to the bottle of vodka and leave at room temperature for a day or so to allow the lemon to infuse the vodka, before freezing.

Leave it for a few more days, if you can, before drinking, for the lemon flavour to further infuse the vodka.

bits, bobs & basics

Some useful tips, accompaniments, frills and embellishments that will hopefully become useful additions to your repertoire.

griddled bread

Diagonally slice a country-style loaf of bread such as ciabatta about 1 cm (½ in) thick, and rub both sides with olive oil and some sea salt. Heat a griddle pan until very hot and griddle the bread on both sides until it is golden and little charred with stripes across the middle. The bread can be griddled several hours ahead, put on a baking sheet and reheated for a few minutes just before required.

making breadcrumbs

I use both fresh and dried breadcrumbs; you'll find them in the following recipes: Stuffed Marrow (squash) (page 60), Beef or Lamb and Harissa Rissoles with Tomato Sauce (page 54), Italian Meatballs with Tomato Sauce (page 92), Lamb's Liver Schnitzel (page 70) and Spicy Sausage, Lamb and Bean Bake (page 109).
Fresh breadcrumbs Remove and discard the crusts from a two-day-old white loaf and process into fine crumbs. Freeze in a polythene bag. They freeze beautifully and don't compact when frozen, making them easy to extract in small amounts.
Dried breadcrumbs Completely dry out stale bits of white bread and rolls in a very low or cooling oven. Process into fine crumbs and store in a lidded container where they will last almost indefinitely. There is no need to freeze them. Try not to use too many dark crusts, or brown the bread at all whilst drying out, as this will result in brown crumbs, rather than the whiteish pale biscuit colour that you are after.

grating parmesan

Grating fresh Parmesan cheese is a bit of a labour of love using a domestic grater, especially if any quantity is required. So, I chop a large block into chunks and grate it using the grater disc of a food processor. I then swap the disc for the chopping blade and process until the Parmesan is very fine. Then pop it into a plastic bag or box and freeze. The cheese stays crumbly when frozen so you can just spoon out as much as you need and use it straight away.

reheating rice

Rice can be cooked up to a day in advance and reheated when required. However, it is prone to develop bacteria which can cause food poisoning if it is not cooled properly or if left at room temperature for any length of time. Follow these tips carefully for a really good get-ahead trick to have up your sleeve.

Cool cooked rice immediately by tipping into a sieve and running cold water through it until completely cold. Stick a few draining holes through it using your fingers and leave to drain for a few minutes. Spread into a shallow ovenproof serving dish no deeper than 5 cm (2 in), which allows the rice to reheat evenly all the way through. Cover and refrigerate immediately.

Reheat thoroughly. Splash with a little water, cover with foil and heat in a preheated oven 180°C (350°F) gas 4 for 20–30 minutes, stirring gently halfway, until completely hot all the way through. Alternatively, cover with boiling water, stir to separate the grains and drain. Or add a splash of water, cover with damp paper towel and microwave for a minute or two, stirring half-way through.

pickled cucumber

Finely slice 1 cucumber, preferably using a mandolin and mix with 2 heaped teaspoons of sugar, 4 tablespoons of white wine vinegar and a sprinkling of salt. Leave to stand for an hour or two, giving it the odd stir from time to time. Sweet, sour, savoury and good with so many cold starters.

GET AHEAD
This will last for several days in the fridge.

cucumber raita

Peel 1 large cucumber with a potato peeler and shave the flesh into long strips, discarding the core of seeds in the middle. Cut the strips roughly into chunks, place in a colander, sprinkle with a little salt and leave to drain for 30 minutes.

Squeeze out the excess liquid, mix with 500 g (1 lb 2 oz) yoghurt, season with salt, if needed, and pepper and spoon into a serving bowl. Use as a dip or a sauce – it's excellent for cooling down spicy food.

GET AHEAD
Make up to 2 days in advance, cover and chill.

balsamic syrup

This thickened vinegar is delicious drizzled over a wide variety of starters, savoury tarts and salads. Boil some balsamic vinegar rapidly in a small saucepan until it is reduced by about half. It should have become slightly syrupy but bear in mind that it will thicken up considerably when cold and will not be as thick and syrupy in the pan.

mint sauce

Chop a bunch of fresh mint leaves and mix in a small bowl with 1 tbsp granulated sugar and a pinch of salt. Pour over boiling water to barely cover and stir until the sugar has dissolved. Add white wine vinegar to taste, around 3–4 tablespoons.

Mint

raspberry vinegar

Put 450 g (1 lb) fresh or frozen raspberries into a bowl and add 570 ml (1 pint) of red or white wine vinegar. Cover and leave in a cool place for 4 days.

Strain through a piece of muslin, a jelly bag or a few layers of paper towel lining a sieve. Measure the liquid and pour into a saucepan. For every 570 ml (1 pint) of liquid add 225 g (8 oz) of granulated sugar. Bring slowly to the boil, stirring occasionally with a wooden spoon to help the sugar dissolve and simmer for 15 minutes.

Pour into sterilised bottles or jars (see page 186) and seal. This will keep for months, if not years, and is very good in salad dressings and drizzled over cold starters, as well as with roast pork (see page 68).

HINTS AND TIPS
The vinegar improves in flavour and becomes more syrupy with age. In an elegantly shaped bottle, it makes a lovely present for friends.

Raspberries

tapenade croûtes

Preheat the oven to 200°C (400°F) gas 6. Take 1 small baguette, sourdough, ciabatta, bloomer or country-style loaf and slice thinly. Spread each slice with a covering of tapenade. Snip into fingers, or the shape of your choice, using scissors. Cook on a baking sheet for 5–10 minutes. Transfer to a wire cooling rack.

Try one of these toppings: chopped red (bell) pepper mixed with capers and parsley or basil; quails' eggs and anchovy; tomato salsa; buffalo mozzarella and a ribbon of Parma ham; goats' cheese and chopped walnuts.

tomato vinaigrette

Liquidise 225 g (8 oz) very ripe tomatoes and and sieve into a bowl. Whisk in a large pinch of caster (superfine granulated) sugar, a little white wine vinegar, 4–8 tablespoons of olive oil and season with salt and freshly ground black pepper. Check the seasoning – you may want to adjust and add a little more of something. This is a delicious and pretty accompaniment for many starters, grilled or fried fish and chicken. The vinaigrette will keep happily in the fridge for several days.

roasted red (bell) pepper sauce

Preheat the oven to 220°C (425°F) gas 7. Quarter and deseed 3 red (bell) peppers and then place skin side up, on a baking sheet lined with foil or silicone paper. Cook until beginning to char and blacken around the edges. This will take about 20 minutes.

When cool enough to handle, slide off the skins and discard. Process or liquidise the peppers into a smooth sauce with ¼ tsp salt, freshly ground black pepper, 1 small chopped clove of garlic, a splash of lemon juice, some olive oil and a little white wine vinegar. Check the seasoning and adjust the ingredients accordingly. A fabulous, jewel-coloured sauce that is delicious with tarts, aspargus, chicken or fish.

GET AHEAD
Make several days ahead and keep covered in the fridge. The sauce improves with age and will keep for weeks in the fridge. To save time you can use a jar of ready-roasted (bell) peppers.

stuffed mediterranean ciabatta

This is just too good! Perfect picnic food and delicious with cold meats or as an accompaniment to soup for lunch.

Serves 12–15

500 g (1 lb 2 oz) packet ciabatta
*   bread mix*
2–3 tbsp pesto (see page 183)
½ x 280-g (10-oz) jar sun-dried
*   or sun-blush tomatoes*
½ x 280-g (10-oz) jar chargrilled
*   artichokes in oil*
½ x 280-g (10 oz) jar roast red (bell)
*   peppers*

12 black olives, pitted and sliced
110 g (4 oz) Taleggio cheese, cut
*   roughly into small dice*
a few sprigs of fresh thyme or rosemary
thinly sliced red onion (optional)
sea salt
olive oil

GET AHEAD
Prepare the filling ingredients up to two days ahead, cover and chill.

Artichokes

Tip the bread mix into a processor or electric mixer fitted with its dough blade/hook and make a dough according to the instructions on the packet. I use slightly less liquid than suggested, so instead of 350 ml (12½ fl oz) I use 330 ml (11 fl oz). This gives a slightly less sticky wet dough, which is easier to work with. Knead in the processor for a few minutes or as long as you dare, keeping hold of the processor as it tends to walk! A damp dishcloth underneath helps.

Roll the dough out on a well-floured surface until it is approximately 46 x 36 cm (14 x 18 in). This is just a rough guide. Lift half of the dough onto a large flat baking sheet lined with silicone paper. Make sure there is plenty of flour under the dough left on the work surface to stop it sticking. Spread the half on the baking sheet with pesto, then roughly snip the tomatoes, artichokes and peppers over the pesto. Scatter over half the olives and most of the Taleggio, reserving a little for the top.

Fold the plain dough over the filling as though closing a book and press the edges together well. Make indentations in the top with your fingers and scatter over the rest of the olives, the Taleggio, thyme or rosemary sprigs and red onion, if using, and some sea salt. Finally, drizzle over a little olive oil. Cover loosely with clingfilm and leave somewhere warm for 30–45 minutes or until it has doubled in size and feels spongy.

Meanwhile preheat the oven to 200°C (400°F) gas 6. Cook for 10–15 minutes or until golden brown. Slide onto a wire rack to cool a little. Serve warm or cold.

soda bread

The classic Irish bread is one of the simplest breads to make as it contains no yeast. Delicious with starters, particularly smoked salmon or any smoked fish; with cheese, soup and cold meats, or just with butter and jam.

Makes 1 round loaf

225 g (8 oz) plain (all-purpose) flour
225 g (8 oz) wholemeal flour
1 tsp bicarbonate of soda (baking soda)
2 tsp cream of tartar
1 tbsp caster (superfine granulated)
   sugar

1 tsp salt
1 tbsp olive oil
225 g (8 oz) natural yoghurt
200 ml (7 fl oz) milk

Preheat the oven to 190°C (375°F) gas 5. In a large bowl sift together the flours, bicarbonate of soda, cream of tartar, sugar and salt.

Mix together the olive oil and yoghurt and stir into the dry ingredients with a wooden spoon. Add enough milk to make a soft dough. You may not need it all. Knead together gently with your hands, in the bowl, just to bring it together and no more, as overworking makes it tough. If you prefer, make the bread in a processor but only process just enough to bring the dough together using the pulse button.

Put onto a baking sheet and shape into a round. Press the handle of a wooden spoon down lengthways into the top of the dough to form a cross or wedge shapes. Dust with a little wholemeal flour and bake in the preheated oven for 30–45 minutes. When cooked, the loaf will sound hollow when tapped on the bottom. Leave to cool on a wire rack.

VARIATION

Try making a walnut soda bread. Simply add 170 g (6 oz) chopped walnuts to the dry ingredients and 1 tbsp of walnut oil to the wet ingredients. As well as being particularly good with cheese, walnut bread makes an excellent base for canapés. Slice thickly, cut out small round croûtes with a pastry cutter, put on a baking sheet, scatter with a little sea salt and olive oil and cook until just brown and crispy.

pesto

Pesto really needs no introduction. However, I will say that pesto bought in jars bears absolutely no resemblance to the homemade real thing.

Serves 6–8 as a pasta sauce

50 g (2 oz) fresh basil leaves
   (about 85 g/3 oz on the stem)
½ tsp salt
2 cloves of garlic, roughly sliced

50 g (2 oz) pine nuts
50 g (2 oz) freshly grated Parmesan
125 ml (4 fl oz) olive oil

GET AHEAD
The pesto keeps for months in the fridge and also freezes perfectly. Just remember to make sure it is submerged under a slick of olive oil at the top of the jar to stop it discolouring. Every time you spoon some out of the jar, level the pesto off and cover with more oil.

Process the basil and salt together then add the garlic and pine nuts. Process again until the mixture becomes a chunky paste.

Add the Parmesan and process until well blended. Very slowly add the olive oil with the processor running, until the mixture has a creamy texture. More or less oil can be added depending on the consistency required. Check the seasoning – you might like to add a little more salt.

Pour into a sterilised jar (see page 186), level the top with a teaspoon and pour over a slick of olive oil to seal the pesto until required.

Basil

foaming hollandaise

This is just fantastic, especially for those frightened of making the notoriously easy-to-curdle regular hollandaise. It will not curdle as its cousin is prone to do if overheated or reheated, because the egg whites stabilise it. It is also much lighter, goes further and can be made in advance. Delicious with fish, poached eggs, artichokes and asparagus.

Serves 8–12

2 tbsp white wine vinegar
2 eggs, separated, plus 1 yolk

salt and freshly ground black pepper
225 g (8 oz) butter

Put the vinegar into a small saucepan and boil rapidly until reduced by half.

Put the egg yolks and a little salt and pepper into the bowl of a food processor and with the motor running, slowly pour the vinegar over the yolks in a thin stream. The yolks will thicken up.

Melt the butter gently in the same pan and with the motor running, very slowly pour it onto the yolk mixture in a thin stream. Scrape the sauce into a good-sized mixing bowl.

Whisk the egg whites with a pinch of salt in a separate bowl until fairly stiff but not dry. Stir a spoonful of whites into the sauce, to soften the mixture, before carefully folding in the rest. Pour into a serving bowl.

GET AHEAD
Make up to 3 days in advance, cool, cover and keep in the fridge or freeze.

HINTS AND TIPS
To warm through, bring back to room temperature several hours before required, then 15–30 minutes or so before needed suspend over a pan of hot water. If you have an Aga, sit the bowl on a folded tea towel somewhere warm on the top. It will sit quite happily for a long time.

To use from frozen, thaw at room temperature and then follow the method above.

Bear in mind that hollandaise by nature cannot be served hot – nor is it meant to be – just warm. With the addition of egg whites it warms through in minutes as there is no density to it.

Artichokes

salsa verde

This classic flavour-packed green sauce is very good with so many things – grilled, poached or fried fish and meats.

Salsa verde – the remains!

Serves 8

6 anchovies
1 tbsp capers
1 tbsp cocktail gherkins
1 clove of garlic
2 large handfuls of parsley leaves
1 handful of mint leaves (optional)

1 tbsp lemon juice
1 tbsp Dijon mustard
8 tbsp olive oil
salt and freshly ground black pepper

Either blitz the first six ingredients together in a small food processor, making sure that you don't over-process them into a paste, or chop them by hand. Transfer to a bowl and stir in the rest of the ingredients. Check the seasoning.

HINTS AND TIPS
Use other soft green herbs as well, if you have them to hand, such as tarragon, basil or chervil. It will keep happily for several days although the bright green colour will fade a little.

tomato, shallot and parsley salsa

This salsa goes with, and lifts, so many things, particularly grilled, griddled, fried or barbecued fish, meat and poultry.

Serves 6

300 g (10½ oz) small, very ripe tomatoes
2 shallots, finely chopped
large handful of curly parsley, roughly chopped

1 green chilli (chili pepper), seeded and finely chopped
½ tsp sugar
salt and freshly ground black pepper
1 tbsp balsamic vinegar

Cut the tomatoes into quarters and then each quarter in half horizontally. Put into a bowl and stir in the rest of the ingredients. The salsa needs to be well seasoned so check the seasoning and be generous with the salt and pepper.

HINTS AND TIPS
Make at least 1 hour in advance to allow the flavours to develop. Add a little more balsamic vinegar if the tomatoes are not juicy enough. Tomatoes are best stored at room temperature.

oven-dried tomatoes

Oven-dried tomatoes have a deep, concentrated, savoury flavour and are an excellent way of preserving seasonal gluts. They are delicious added to soups, stews, sauces, salads, starters and pasta. How much or how little you dry them is up to you. Leave them in the oven until completely dried and wrinkled or remove them when still a little plump and fleshy. If you are drying a large quantity leave the oven door ajar to let out the excess steam which is created by the large volume.

tomatoes
fine salt
freshly ground black pepper

dried oregano
caster (superfine granulated) sugar
extra virgin olive oil

HINTS AND TIPS
To sterilise jars wash them well in soapy water and dry, then either run them through a dishwasher cycle, heat for 20 minutes in an oven preheated to 180°C (350°F) gas 4 or microwave (as long as they have no metal bits!) for 2 minutes with a little water in the bottom.

Preheat the oven to 100°C (200°F) gas ½.

Slice the tomatoes in half, through the equator, as it were. Place cut side up on a wire cake rack and suspend over a roasting tin or baking sheet, to catch any drips. Sprinkle with a little salt, black pepper, oregano and sugar. Leave in the oven for between 3–8 hours. The timing depends on how large or juicy the tomatoes are and how dry you want the finished product.

Remove from the oven and leave to cool before packing them tightly into well-sterilised Kilner (Mason) or jam jars. Fill the jars up with extra-virgin olive oil, making sure that the tomatoes are all submerged and cover with the lid. This is very important as they will go mouldy otherwise. Store in the fridge for several months.

index

about the author

Jane Lovett has always been passionate about food, cooking and all things culinary. Describing herself as 'greedy and thinking about food most of the time', she says as soon as she's finished one meal, she's thinking about, and planning, the next.

Having obtained a diploma from the Cordon Bleu Cookery School in London, Jane worked at Leith's Good Food in the City of London, moving on to teach at Leith's School of Food and Wine. She started her own business, providing innovative food for private parties and companies such as *The Economist* and *Vogue*. She has worked as a food stylist and tested and developed recipes for many cookbooks.

Nowadays Jane gives cookery demonstrations from her home in beautiful rural North Northumberland, as well as London and other parts of Britain. Her fresh modern approach, tips, shortcuts and original ideas appeal to novice and experienced cooks alike. Her mission is to teach home cooks that cooking is easier than they think, to inspire and instill the confidence to unlock their own skill.

Jane writes a regular monthly food column for *The Northumbrian* magazine and has been featured in other publications. She lives with her husband, John, and has three children. She loves rural life and as a keen gardener, enjoys growing and cooking her own fruit and vegetables.

Visit Jane at her website, *www.janelovett.com*.